Does American Democracy Still Work?

Does American Democracy Still Work?

ALAN WOLFE

Yale University Press   New Haven and London

The Future of American Democracy series aims to examine,
sustain, and renew the historic vision of American democracy
in a series of books by some of America's foremost thinkers.
The books in the series present a new, balanced, centrist
approach to examining the challenges American democracy
has faced in the past and must overcome in the years ahead.

Series editor: Norton Garfinkle.

Set in Minion type by Integrated Publishing Solutions, Grand Rapids, Michigan.
Printed in the United States of America by R. R. Donnelley, Harrisonburg, Virginia.

Library of Congress Cataloging-in-Publication Data
Wolfe, Alan, 1942–
Does American democracy still work? / Alan Wolfe.
    p.   cm.—(The future of American democracy)
Includes bibliographical references and index.
ISBN-13: 978-0-300-10859-0 (cloth : alk. paper)
ISBN-10: 0-300-10859-1 (cloth : alk. paper)
1. Democracy—United States.   2. United States—Politics and government.
I. Title.   II. Series
JK1726.W65   2006
320.973—dc22   2006008116

A catalogue record for this book is available from the British Library.

The paper in this book meets the guidelines for permanence and durability of the
Committee on Production Guidelines for Book Longevity of the Council on Library
Resources.

10 9 8 7 6 5 4 3 2 1

Contents

Acknowledgments

Jonathan Brent of Yale University Press was an enthusiastic backer of this book from the moment I proposed it to him. Along with his assistant Sarah Miller, he made Yale a wonderful partner for this venture. I am also grateful to my literary agent Fredi Friedman for making the match.

Three anonymous readers for the Press offered helpful suggestions, as did one who revealed his name. Since this last one was someone I have long admired and welcomed as a friend, I want to extend special thanks to Sandy Levinson for his advice over many decades—yes, decades.

Norton Garfinkle and Patrick Glynn of the Future of American Democracy Foundation have been strong supporters of this book, as has been Amitai Etzioni. My thanks to them all.

As usual, my family makes it all possible.

I

The New Politics of Democracy

S truggles over American democracy were easier to understand in the nineteenth and twentieth century than
they have become in the twenty-first. Then, privileged
elites—would-be aristocrats in the North, slaveholders
in the South, the wealthy everywhere—opposed democracy,
and for the simplest of motivations: the more restricted the
franchise, the greater the likelihood these elites would hold on
to their unfairly gained advantages. For the same reason, if in
reverse, groups marginalized by the priorities of their era—
working people, women, racial minorities—wished democracy expanded to shift the benefits provided by government in
their direction. In the old politics of democracy, the left spoke
on behalf of the people, while the right tended to the business
of the powerful.[1] The differences between them were many,
but they were mostly economic. Those who wanted to restrict
the scope of politics, as E. E. Schattschneider pointed out in
1960, emphasized "individualism, free private enterprise, lo-
calism, privacy, and economy in government," while those intent on expanding it insisted on "equal protection of the laws,

justice, liberty, freedom of movement, freedom of speech and association, and civil rights."[2]

One can still find traces of the old politics of democracy in American life. Liberals frequently insist that America is not democratic enough: many convicted felons are denied the suffrage; difficulties in obtaining citizenship render numerous immigrants unable to vote on matters affecting their lives; too many Americans who have the right to vote fail to exercise it; voting machines, let alone supposedly nonpartisan state officials, do not always work, especially in minority communities; some states—including Georgia, which recently passed a law requiring a driver's license or its equivalent in order to vote— hark back to the days when voting was more of a privilege than a right; the U.S. Constitution guarantees disproportionate numbers of U.S. Senate seats to states with small populations; and the electoral college has chosen the popular-vote loser too many times for anyone's comfort.[3] Clearly there is some justice in these claims; democratic institutions, for all their widespread appeal to contemporary Americans, rarely live up to the standard of one person, one vote.

In contrast to liberals, who traditionally have held to the conviction that more democracy is better democracy, the charge is sometimes launched by conservatives that America is too democratic for its own good; what is popular is not always what is right, they from time to time remind us, and a society that bases its most important decisions on what appeals to the lowest common denominator is likely to reach the wrong ones.[4] For these traditionalists, democracy is inappropriate in any area of life, such as culture or religion, but it is especially wrong-headed in politics; in the extreme case, totalitarianism is not the opposite of democracy but the logical extension of populist instincts run wild.[5] Conservative skeptics of democracy are unlikely to get much of a mass hearing for their claims; most media, including most forms of book publishing, appeal to the very popular taste that curmudgeons of this sort disdain. Still, no matter how democratic America's institutions have become, skepticism on the right end of the political spectrum has not completely disappeared.

For all the talk of expanding democracy on one side and curtailing it on the other, however, the old politics of democracy no longer inspires much passion. Hindering the left's case is the fact that democracy has gone about as far as it can go; now that nearly all adults have the right to vote, it is no longer possible to alter significantly today's political balance of power by trying to bring tomorrow's new groups of players into the contest.[6] Any proposed changes to make the Constitution more democratic, moreover, run up against the resistance of small states, which would lose power; even as committed an enthusiast of democracy as Robert A. Dahl concedes his "measured pessimism" when it comes to formal reforms that would make the United States a more democratic society.[7] Denying those who wish to vote their right to do so is reason for indignation, but such incidents, even in today's highly polarized electoral climate, are more the exception than the rule. It can hardly be a coincidence that the left so often comes across as tired and defensive; it threw so much of its energy into gaining the right to vote that it does not know where to turn once the vote has been gained.

Conservatives, as it happens, no longer speak in the old language of democracy either. In sharp contrast to their previous skepticism toward the masses, conservatives today are engaged in a love fest of praise for ordinary people. For this, they can hardly be blamed; there are—and for some time have been—more conservatives than liberals in America, and even if it is also true that there are more moderates than both of them, the right-leaning political instincts of the American public constitute a brute fact that American liberals, perhaps for understandable reasons, have been reluctant to accept.[8] American conservatives are not happy campers: looking out on the society in which they live, they see decadence all around them and, quick to identify themselves as victims, they claim, with greater and greater implausibility, that liberals still run the United States of America. But on the issue of democracy, the state of American public opinion offers them undeniable advantages; American political history and culture are rich in democratic rhetoric, and the side that appeals convincingly to ordinary people will always have an advantage compared with the side that appeals to elites, tradition, leadership, habit, deference, restraint, rules, judges, or wisdom. Why, if you are a contemporary conservative, bite the hand that feeds you? Expanding the scope of the electorate once seemed a threat to your interests; now it seems the perfect way to get what you want.

The United States, in short, has entered into a new politics of democracy. Two features make the new politics of democracy different from earlier struggles over the extension of the franchise or debates over the purposes and reach of government. The first is that the major divisions between left and right are not over economics but, as the frequently used term "culture war" implies, over moral and religious issues. The second is that the side that wins—most frequently in contemporary politics, the right side—is the one that best frames its appeals in the language of populism.

Neither moralism nor populism is new in American public life; if anything, both of them have been prominent features of American politics since the nineteenth century. The Civil War was, in large part, a bitter conflict over moral values framed, on both sides, by the language of religion. Late-nineteenth-century politics not only featured a Populist Party but was dominated by the three presidential campaigns of William Jennings Bryan, who defined the very meaning of populism. Yet moralism and populism, at least until very recently, rarely worked together. At the time of the Civil War, the majority of Americans did not have the right to vote (one reason the war was fought in the first place), placing severe limits on how populistic the crusades around it could be. And Bryan's populist presidential campaigns, which took the form of crusades, were primarily concerned with economic issues, such as the free coinage of silver and the tariff. Only with the arrival of the culture war in the 1970s—accompanied by such democratizing features of American life as the increasing sophistication of polling and the spread of cable television—did moralism and populism work together to transform the very character of American democracy.

Both features of the new politics of democracy were, at least at first, fueled by the energies of the political left. This was certainly true of the culture war. *Roe v. Wade* (1973) or the U.S. Senate's rejection of Robert Bork (1987) is often cited as the moment at which the culture war began; both events symbolized the willingness of the left to put moral issues front and center in American public attention. For numerous liberal political activists, the culture war was equivalent to a good business plan; they could raise money and energize supporters by proclaiming their steadfast devotion to a woman's right to choose or their equally steadfast opposition to a theocracy led by a Jerry Falwell or a Pat Robertson. To this day, a preference persists on the left for culture war politics; the moment a Republican president nominates a conservative judge—especially one such as Samuel Alito, who, during his confirmation hearings for a seat on the U.S. Supreme Court, refused to concede that *Roe v. Wade* was settled law—liberal groups swing into determined opposition.

In the longer run, however, the culture war turned out to be a gift to the right. Even though public opinion is frequently not as hostile to a woman's right to choose as those on the right convince themselves, conservatives are far more likely to win elections by emphasizing their religious faith and strong sense of right and wrong than they are by insisting on their relatively unpopular budgetary nostrums, such as increasing spending on Arctic oil drilling while reducing it for first responders.[9] It was, after all, not only Democrats who brought up the subject of abortion during the hearings to confirm Samuel Alito; Republican Senators such as Tom Coburn of Oklahoma and Sam Brownback of Kansas did so as well, and truth be told, in their opposition to *Roe v. Wade* they showed far more passion than did Democrats, whose support for a woman's right to choose, especially in comparison with the Bork hearings a decade and a half earlier, seemed not only less demagogic but more perfunctory.

The passion of Senators Coburn and Brownback reflects a political reality in which Republicans have taken the lead in talking about stem cells, God, and the culture of life, while Democrats want politics to focus on such policy-wonkish issues as the minimum wage or global warming. Especially on Fox News, the television station most closely guided by conservative talking points, liberals are routinely portrayed as out to destroy Christmas, keep God out of the schools and off the coins, and wield the club of political correctness to deny conservatives their rights to free speech. Even foreign policy issues are treated by Republicans in culture war terms; instead of speaking as a realist in the aftermath of September 11, President Bush presented global conflict as a struggle between good and evil. And as befits a foreign policy steeped in moral language, he relied extensively on the emotion of fear to justify programs, such as unauthorized wiretapping or extensive executive power, that might otherwise be viewed as violations of civil liberty or attacks on the principle of separation of powers.

Such culture war appeals do not always work to the benefit of Republicans and conservatives. Despite the right's effort to rally the country around the cause of Terri Schiavo, a brain-dead Florida woman, few Americans seemed interested in transforming her tragic situation into a political football. No moral crusading, moreover, whether involving the right to life in domestic politics or the evils of terrorism in foreign policy, helped Mr. Bush as his popularity waned in his second term. Still, even if increasingly ineffective, culture war issues are unlikely to disappear so long as Republicans rely on their conservative Christian base to win elections, a reliance that shows no sign of receding.

The second distinguishing characteristic of the new politics of democracy, the reliance on the rhetoric and techniques of populism, also originally appealed to the left before being adopted by the right. Certainly few presidents have been as sensitive to the realities of polling, and the need to fashion policies to accord with what polling reveals about public opinion, than Bill Clinton. And he is by no means alone; future Democratic candidates will surely seek ways to frame issues by trying to make them more acceptable to the public; indeed, "framing" has become a buzzword attached to liberals as they seek to recover some of the political popularity they have lost.[10] In this they have at least one advantage: Republicans and conservatives frequently manifest an undemocratic side by maintaining strong ties to corporate interests, by asserting

that there exists a "unitary executive" with the authority to ignore legislation duly passed by Congress, and by insisting to an
unusual degree upon secrecy in government.[11] Americans are
not exactly thrilled by the elitist side of Republican policies,
and when that party responds to big business with unstinting
largesse, it enables Democrats to claim, at least in economic
terms, the populistic language that Republicans ignore.

Yet one of the most marked features of recent American
politics is the extent to which populist language and tactics
have worked to benefit the right. Reversing two hundred years
of political rhetoric, liberals are denounced by conservatives as
members of a privileged class, aristocratic in their tastes, con-
temptuous of the choices of ordinary people, determined to
protect their effete lifestyles at all costs, and committed to obtaining their unpopular (and unworkable) objectives through
the most undemocratic means available, while conservatives—
or so the story continues—speak to the heartfelt convictions of
ordinary people for a return to traditional morality, strong and
stable families, and God-fearing American patriotism. In the
new politics of democracy, even Straussian political philosophers, long known as unabashed elitists, call for democracy in
far away places such as Iraq.[12] So widespread is this populist
reflex that it has been adopted by the most undemocratic institution in the modern world; John L. Allen, a keen observer of
the Vatican, has written of the degree to which then-Cardinal
Joseph Ratzinger, later Pope Benedict XVI, "sees himself not as
an inquisitor but as a tribune, protecting ordinary Catholics
from intellectual abuse by self-appointed elites."[13]

No wonder that George W. Bush, for all his talk of ignoring polls, was as relentless in following public opinion, and in
allowing himself to be guided by it, as Bill Clinton. Republicans may be elitist when it comes to rewarding their privileged

constituencies or protecting the powers of the president, but when the focus is on emotional and moral issues, whether the subject involves crime, religion, or national security, they are as populistic in their language as any nineteenth-century advocate for free silver. Republicans were able to gain control over all three branches of government in the early years of the twenty-first century for a reason; they became the more popular party because they became the more populistic party. For conservatives these days, democratic sentiment has become the ultimate trump card for a political ideology that originated as a check on democratic sentiment.

The new politics of democracy constitutes a major turning point in American political history. My business is not predicting political contests, and I have no way of knowing whether conservatives will continue their political dominance or be voted out of office by an electorate that, in the wake of indictments, scandals, unchecked executive power, high energy prices, slow job growth, an unsuccessful war, and revelations of stunning incompetence in the wake of natural disasters, suddenly discovers that perhaps liberalism was not such a bad thing. (This book is being written before the Congressional midterm elections of 2006, in which the Democrats may—or, then again, may not—recapture one or both houses of Congress.) But whichever party governs the United States in the near future, the new politics of democracy is likely to dominate American public life for some time. Elections will be decided, media coverage determined, books written, and policies proposed, not on the basis of which coalitions of forces can bring ever newer groups of people to the polls based on their self-interest, but on the basis of which ones can mobilize those already present in the electorate by speaking to their longings (even as they seek to demobilize those likely to vote against them). The old politics of democracy frequently lacked excitement even though it offered stability. The new politics of democracy is nothing if not exciting, even if the costs are frequent polarization, deadlock, vituperation, and extremism.

The new politics of democracy has been roughly forty years in the making. Conservatives were weak to the point of ridicule after Barry Goldwater's defeat and Lyndon Johnson's victory in 1964, while liberals were strong to the point of arrogance. By 2004 those positions had been reversed: conservatives could barely restrain their triumphalism, and liberals found themselves in the unusual role of being an opposition party.

So dramatic has been the shift from left to right that we sometimes forget that ideology was not the only thing that changed over those years; America's entire way of conducting its political affairs did as well. In 1964 the nominating conventions of both political parties were controlled by party regulars, not dominated by primary voters. Business and its money was a powerful force behind Republicans, but labor and its ability to turn out voters did its best to match that power behind Democrats. To advise them on matters both domestic and foreign, presidents from either party turned to the same East Coast establishment. The South, solidly Democratic, was overrepresented in Congress, but it did not generally determine the outcome of presidential elections; back in those days, it was actually possible for a senator from Massachusetts to be elected president. There were only three major television networks, and the men who ran them exercised significant control over what viewers saw and heard. A seniority system determined who chaired committees in Congress, and Congress conducted much of its business outside the glare of publicity. Bipartisanship was considered a sign of national states-manship, not an indication of unforgivable disloyalty. Political scientists were in near-unanimous agreement that middle-of-the-road campaigns were the most likely to succeed. Ideology had been pronounced dead, as, by the way, had God.

The forces that broke open the consensus-oriented politics of the 1950s and early 1960s were associated with the left. Shaken by the assassinations of the Kennedy brothers and Martin Luther King, Jr., distraught by the war in Vietnam, convinced that the United States was doing a poor job overcoming its racial, sexual, and class divisions, the New Left's call for participatory democracy shattered the traditions and practices that enabled elites to run most of America's institutions relatively unchecked. Pushed by crusading liberal reformers, democracy expanded its reach. "Between the late 1950s and early 1970s," the historian Alexander Keyssar has written, "the legal underpinnings of the right to vote were transformed more dramatically than they had been at any earlier point in the nation's history."[14] So democratic was the spirit of the time that courts ruled that homeless people had a right to vote, their place of residence defined as the park benches on which they slept. Within the course of one generation's experience, the United States went from imagining itself as a democracy in theory to becoming one in practice.

Yet if the original democratic energy came from the left, it would more than spill over to benefit the right. Over the longer haul, conservatives simply outhustled liberals. They developed better political networks. They won important wars of ideas. Their sense of purpose was stronger and their determination remarkable. If they could not take over institutions dominated by liberals and moderates, they created their own, run by conservatives. Churches that evangelized in search of new members with spirit and enthusiasm grew; those that emphasized theological liberalism and more staid forms of worship did not. With the (significant) exception of California, states that once had weak political parties and histories of direct democracy turned right; those that had more established parties run by elites stayed left. Regions of the country that were gaining residents became Republican; those losing them were more likely to be Democratic. In the wake of this great conservative success, liberals who believe in the necessity of political organizing look to the rise of the conservative movement to find what is missing on their own side of the political ledger.[15]

Democracy as it was practiced in 1964 was anything but perfect; there is not much to admire about senators from one-party states holding seats for life, urban political machines rife with corruption, East Coast Republicans unaware that the base of their party was shifting to the West and South, or widespread media censorship enforced by a lack of competition. In challenging that way of doing public business, the new politics of democracy shook up a system that had grown fat and lazy, and for that, Americans of all political persuasions should be grateful. Populist appeals, whether focused on economic issues, as they were in the nineteenth and twentieth centuries, or moral and religious ones, as they are in the twenty-first, bring with them distinct advantages; matters of deep concern to ordinary people cannot be swept under the rug by politicians intent on conducting inside-the-beltway business. No longer run by political barons protected by seniority, arcane rules, noncompetitive media, and a bipartisan willingness to divide the spoils, the United States is in many ways as democratic as it has ever been in its history. If democracy consisted only in the desire of people to express what is on their minds and the willingness of their leaders to respond to those desires, American democracy today would be a cause for celebration.

Populism, moreover, is here to stay. So successful have conservatives and Republicans been at claiming the populist mantle that Democrats and liberals feel little choice but to respond in kind; Bryan's populism, once derided by historians on the left because of the Great Commoner's stance during the Scopes trial, is now viewed sympathetically, his synthesis of economic justice and religious conviction offering an appealing formula for the contemporary Democratic Party.[16] And it is not only in the United States where populism rules the roost; in 2005 voters in France and Holland made very clear the degree to which they opposed the plans for a European constitution advocated by their leaders. We live in democratic times, and this, as the British sociologist Frank Furedi has written, is bound to be uncomfortable for anyone claiming special wisdom, especially including intellectuals, who typically distrust populism because it allows so little space for them to use their presumably superior intelligence.[17]

Still, populism, whether in Europe or the United States, has always been accompanied by troubling tendencies toward demagoguery and emotionalism. In its left-wing form, populism flirted with anti-Semitism and anti-Catholicism and embraced, as the life of Bryan demonstrates, overt racism. In its right-wing form, as the political analyst Anatol Lieven has suggested, populism lines up naturally with xenophobia, Christian triumphalism, and anti-intellectualism.[18] Intellectuals should not, therefore, feel barred from raising questions about populist democracy just because they live in states where the weather is cold, drink French wine rather than American beer, rarely watch television, and inevitably vote for losers. Because of both moralism and populism, the new politics of democracy raises uncomfortable questions about how well democracy is working.

The most troubling of those questions is whether the quality of democratic life has improved as the quantity of democratic life has expanded. Democracy, it is important to remember, does have qualitative dimensions as well as quantitative ones; its health is measured not only by how many are eligible to vote but by how many actually do, how much knowledge they bring to their decisions, how responsive they and their leaders are to the common good, whether their participation leaves them feeling satisfied or frustrated, the degree to which the decisions their leaders make are wise, the extent to which those leaders promote policies that advance social justice and strengthen the common good, and the ways in which politicians can be held accountable for the decisions they reach. Before we can pass judgment on the state of American democracy, we must address not only how far it reaches but whether the way it operates brings out the best in Americans and their society.

In the chapters that follow I will review evidence accumulated by political scientists which suggests that, when it comes to the quality of its performance, American democracy is not doing well at all. Voters, for one thing, know very little about politics, a fact that may not have mattered much when politics was more consensual but matters greatly when politics is more ideological, campaigns more expensive and nasty, and policies as polarizing as they are popular. There are, as well, serious problems of accountability in American political life; even criteria once viewed as the bare minimum necessary to hold political leaders accountable for their decisions, such as competitive elections, are withering away. In the absence of effective accountability, legislation in Congress is increasingly passed without input from the minority party and in ways contrary to traditional rules about deliberation and debate, while the executive branch, oblivious to the concept of the separation of powers, acts as if, once an election is over, its decisions are no longer subject to review. A well-functioning democracy requires the existence of strong institutions such as political parties and interest groups, yet the tendency of Americans to view such institutions with suspicion paradoxically fuels partisanship, encourages rampant corruption, and strengthens the hands of political elites. To avoid endless cycles of partisan retaliation, political systems are dependent on the existence of neutral bodies such as courts, the media, or administrative experts, yet neutrality is also a fast-disappearing feature of contemporary American political life; in the extreme case, the distinction between politics and policy vanishes completely as the art of governance is used to promote the goals of the party that governs. And as politics, in the absence of neutral referees, becomes a war of all against other, those who suffer most are those with the fewest resources, severing a link between democratic ideals and the pursuit of social justice with potentially serious implications for the long-term stability of society at home and a global system of international understandings abroad.

If this evidence accumulated by political scientists is taken seriously, as I believe it ought to be, Americans should be as proud of their democracy's expansion as they are concerned about its actual operations. "Although the formal right to vote is now nearly universal," Alexander Keyssar concludes, "few observers would characterize the United States as a vibrant democracy, as a nation where the equality of political rights offers release to a host of engaged and diverse political voices."[19] To America's great credit, democracy exists, and any American can take advantage of its benefits. And to America's great shame, all too many Americans have become passive spectators in the hurly-burly of democratic politics, unwilling to play much of a role in its operations, yet ever ready to complain when it fails to meet their needs.

As important as it may be to address questions of democratic performance, the new politics of democracy does not make it easy. In earlier periods of American history, factory workers and immigrants, frequently helped along by labor unions and urban political machines, rushed to become voters, and it became the task of society's more respectable and conservative sectors to point out how corrupt those organizations were and to urge reforms that would ensure their honesty. Based on majority rule, the old politics of democracy did not bypass entirely those conservatives who spoke for privileged minorities. Such conservatives were the conscience of the country. It was up to them to insist that democracy could retain a place for nonpartisan expertise and administrative responsibility, no matter how unpopular those ideals might be, in a world of patronage and graft, no matter how widespread those realities had become.

Under the rules of the new politics of democracy, by contrast, conservatives receive such pronounced benefits from their populistic and moral crusades that they are not about to engage in any reforms likely to bring voters to the polls irrespective of their political views, insist on neutral rules applicable to all, limit the ubiquity of negative campaigning, hold politicians accountable for their decisions, or overcome cynicism toward Washington and its way of conducting the people's business. The enthusiastic endorsement by conservatives of a majoritarianism they once disdained has changed the tone of American politics. If the price to be paid for political influence includes turning away from such traditionally conservative ideals as the rule of law, the weight of tradition, commitment to principle, skepticism toward popular culture, fiscal and judicial restraint, and the use of political office as a bully pulpit, contemporary conservatives will gladly pay it. Efforts to stand above the fray or to take the long view, after all, are a product of a period in which conservatives, outflanked by the ability of their liberal opponents to bring ever-larger numbers to the polls, typically lost most of the elections they contested, and no one—at least not these days—enters politics in order to lose. The recently discovered ability of conservatism to attract large numbers of voters to its side resolves a long-standing tension within the right between its insistence on high standards and its willingness to cut corners; nearly all traces of the former have disappeared as the latter becomes the operating principle of presidential and legislative politics. Conservatism no longer stands as a bulwark against instant gratification, and because it does not, the conservatism we lack is a greater threat to democracy than the conservatism we have.

All of which leaves the task of focusing on the qualitative problems of the new politics of democracy to others, including independents who respect process and tradition, moderates seeking a return to a more bipartisan era of cooperation, and liberals who find themselves on the losing end of America's political popularity contests. The last of these will not find it easy to raise questions of democratic quality for two reasons. One is that liberals and Democrats received disproportionate benefits from democracy's qualitative failures in the past, just as Republicans are receiving them today. It was not the lofty rhetoric of an Adlai Stevenson or John F. Kennedy that brought Democrats to the polls in the 1950s and 1960s but the machinations of political bosses like Chicago's Richard Daley. Democratic candidates for president, such as Lyndon B. Johnson, were hardly above negative campaigning and Texas-style electoral shenanigans. One-party politics in the South helped the Democrats control Congress at that time, as did tight rules of procedure and organization that prevented the minority party from exercising much influence. To criticize Republicans now in no way exonerates Democrats then. If American democracy is insufficiently robust, there is plenty of blame to go around.

A second reason why liberals may be hesitant to take on qualitative issues inherent in the new politics of democracy involves the inevitable charge of sour grapes. When liberals did well under modern political conditions, conservatives love to point out, they had no complaints about the system, but now that their candidates so frequently lose, they are suddenly worried about gerrymandering, fund-raising, and negative campaigning, techniques they not only used themselves when in power but perfected as they went along. Democracy requires that the losers accept the winners as legitimate. For liberals to complain about the rules after they begin to lose under them manifests not a desire to improve democracy but an effort to escape its authority. Those searching for evidence that liberals are elitists in sheep's clothing would find in a sudden preoccupation with democracy's qualities all the proof they require.

These are persuasive reasons for a liberal not to take up questions raised about democracy's performance because of the political success of conservatism. Yet in the end, I am not convinced by them.

Conservatives these days may benefit from democracy's qualitative failures more than liberals, but the harms of badly performing democracy are too extensive to be confined only to one political ideology. Those who vote for conservatives may want to believe that taxes can be cut while government spending increases—their leaders, waving magic wands of their own, have not given them reason to think otherwise—but there is a reality out there that trumps every time the political ignorance on which such fantasies are built. Americans concerned with lax moral values can be persuaded to vote for conservative candidates, yet in a political system dependent on raising huge amounts of cash, many of those for whom they vote turn to morally dubious sources—casinos encouraging gambling, pharmaceutical firms selling sexual potency, broadcasters profiting from pornography—that inevitably create cycles of popular disappointment and frustration on the right to match the unhappiness on the left with Democratic politicians who have been forced to move to the center in search of money and votes. Cynicism toward politics helped conservatives when liberals were in power, undermining, as it did, the willingness of the public to support such ambitious legislative reforms as Bill Clinton's health care reform, but when conservatives come to power filled with plans to alter Social Security or to transform the tax code, the same cynicism comes to the aid of liberals dedicated to stopping them. Negative campaigning helps elect conservatives, so much so that it will increasingly be used by conservatives against each other in their internal factional warfare, and struggles over the future leadership of the Republican Party. Any group of Americans with ideas about how their country ought to be run has a stake in improving democracy's quality, not just liberals. However much culture war politics and populism help Republicans as a party, it is not always clear that they benefit conservatives as an ideology, and one of the most fascinating emerging splits in American politics features unhappy advocates of small government and civil liberty dismayed by the tendencies of modern Republicans to produce huge deficits and an all-powerful executive branch.

In addition, as the war in Iraq ought to constantly remind us, democracy is too important a matter to be addressed
through "gotcha" talking points. Had Americans in 2004 reelected the party that took their country into that war based on
a solid understanding of the threat they faced and after a
thoughtful consideration of the war's costs and benefits, we
would be correct to conclude that the lives lost and shattered
by the war, however tragic for the individuals and families involved, were justified in the name of a national objective; no
better system than democracy has ever been invented for determining what those national objectives are and how they
should be realized. But this is not what Americans did. Significant numbers of Americans voted for the war party based on
the factually incorrect premises that Saddam Hussein was responsible for September 11 and that he possessed threatening
weapons of mass destruction. Others agreed with some of
their leaders who claimed, against all principles of democratic
accountability, that support for the country's troops did not
permit critics of the war to have a hearing. Key information
concerning the degree to which political ideology substituted
for good intelligence in the build-up to the war was not revealed until after the reelection of those responsible for it. The
actual details of the fighting—bad decisions, dead bodies, the
strength of the insurgency—were not reported by the media
or were reported too late to have much of an impact. A poorly
functioning democracy honors those who sacrifice their lives
for it less well than a richly working one. Politics involves serious stuff; trivializing it demeans all those affected by its affairs.

Nor, finally, is it wrong to have second thoughts about
democracy's performance after watching it perform. Liberals
have all too often believed that if democracy comes into conflict with liberty—if, for example, large majorities oppose gay
marriage or believe that the words "under God" should remain

in the Pledge of Allegiance—the courts must step in and protect individual rights against majoritarian passions. Their defense of individual rights can be persuasive and moving, but removing issues about which people have strong feelings is also dangerous business, one that can easily lead, in Jack Balkin's strong words, to "elitism, paternalism, authoritarianism, naïveté, excessive and misplaced respect for the 'best and the brightest,' isolation from the concerns of ordinary people, disdain for popular values, fear of popular rule, confusion of factual and moral expertise, and meritocratic hubris."[20] Whatever one thinks of opponents of gay marriage or supporters of the Pledge, they make their case with passion and determination, and it has been based on sincere reflection, moral principle, and appeals to fact. In any democracy worthy of its name, their concerns must be heard and registered.

The picture is quite different, however, when parties to a democratic disagreement take advantage of public ignorance to get their way, lie about their intentions, sneak provisions into legislation after public votes have already been taken, suppress information vital to public debate, and refuse to take responsibility for their actions, all of which, alas, have emerged as features of American democracy as currently practiced. Raising questions about democracy's performance after one's favorite candidates start to lose with depressing regularity may seem to violate democratic norms. But one violates them even more by not addressing transgressions of the rules of democratic life out of the mistaken conviction that those who lose under flawed rules sacrifice their standing to question them.

Improving the performance of American democracy will not be easy; the left, which says it would like to do so, lacks the power, while the right, which has the power, lacks the incentive. Yet America needs a democracy protection movement just as it has an environmental protection movement. It is not just a matter of an electoral college that leads candidates to ignore states in which a large majority of Americans live, campaign finance practices that resemble extortion more than they embody free speech, media that protect those in power rather than hold them responsible for their mistakes, and a Constitution that gives every voter in Wyoming roughly thirty-eight times the influence of every voter in New York State, although all those things are nondemocratic enough. Even if every vote in presidential elections counted equally to every other one, and even if, by some miracle, the political and ideological composition of the U.S. Senate reflected the political and ideological composition of the United States, significant problems of quality control in American democracy would remain.

The natural environment is hearty—often heartier than prophets of environmental doom acknowledge—and it is likely to continue to regenerate itself despite America's relative indifference to its health. Much the same can be said for democracy in America. It has had a long and successful history and it is still here after civil war, two world wars, and the Great Depression. Surely it can and will triumph over its current fascination with morality and populism.

The question Americans face is not whether their society will be democratic but what kind of democracy it will be. And that is very much an open question. Under the twin pressures of culture war issues and populist politics, American democracy is undergoing significant changes that, unless corrected, threaten to undermine some of America's most cherished values, including the liberal values that encourage robust debate, rely on the separation of powers, and recognize the need for a loyal opposition. There is a decided sickness in the American body politic these days which, if not cured, will produce an increasingly angry and divided political class, in the process alienating ever larger numbers of ordinary Americans who will turn away in disgust.

To avoid that fate, Americans are going to have to change their political ways. It is not the case—I wish it were—that voting out Republicans and voting in Democrats will automatically improve the quality of democratic life. Nor will the problems of democratic performance be solved if Congress cleans up its lobbying practices in the wake of the Jack Abramoff scandal, once again turns to campaign finance reform, and resists efforts by the executive branch to aggrandize its power. To begin the process of healing their damaged political environment, Americans will have to pay more attention to the way their elections take place, their laws are passed, and their expectations are shaped. If they do not, American democracy, which in its greatest moments inspired people throughout the world, will lose its luster, destroy the hopes of its founders, and no longer stand as a model for other societies to emulate.

II

Democracy Without Information

Voters are responsible. During political campaigns they process relevant information to make reasonable decisions among the choices presented to them. The views they hold are internally consistent, meaningful, stable over time, and capable of responding to new situations. No wonder, then, that politicians, who risk ignoring public opinion at their own peril, can be held accountable for their performance in office.

These conclusions about how democracy works in the contemporary United States have been reached by an all-star cast of political scientists, including such scholars as V. O. Key, Benjamin Page, Robert Y. Shapiro, Samuel Popkin, and Morris P. Fiorina.[1] Each of them, to one degree or another, is responding to one of the rock-solid findings of empirical political science research: American voters possess scant information about politics and policy. Examples are legion; here are a few. Although Social Security receives ten times the funding of foreign aid, two-thirds of the American people believe the government spends more on foreign aid than on Social Security.[2] Sixty-five percent of Americans in 2003 could not name a single justice of the U.S. Supreme Court, and the best known, the now-retired Sandra Day O'Connor, could be identified by only 25 percent.[3] And in perhaps the most dramatic example of our time, more than 40 percent of Americans continued to believe as late as 2003 that Iraq was deeply involved in the September 11 attack on the United States, even though none of the hijackers was an Iraqi and no collusion between Saddam Hussein and Osama bin Laden has ever been found.[4] Unlike opinion, which is capable of interpretation, information is a straightforward matter; it is either there or it is not. Social Security, the composition of the U.S. Supreme Court, and the war in Iraq are among the dominant issues in American politics in the first decade of the twenty-first century, and it ought to be a cause for concern that correct information about them was either missing or incomplete among the electorate.

On the face of it, gaps in public information would appear to support the conclusions of those, from Alexander Hamilton and Alexis de Tocqueville to Walter Lippmann, who raised questions about whether people would ever be able to live up to the standards that democracy held out for them. Not so, these political scientists point out. For one thing, voters do reason. As Samuel Popkin argues, they may not rely on facts, but they trust gut instinct—Popkin uses the term "low-information rationality"—when making their decisions. Typically they seek out "short-cuts" that stand as surrogates for the positions of those for whom they cast their ballot. In a widely cited example, Popkin points out that Gerald Ford's failure to husk a tamale before trying to eat one on the campaign trail told Mexican Americans all they needed to know about the candidate's ability to understand the problems they faced.

Much the same conclusion emerges from the work of Benjamin Page and Robert Shapiro. Any given voter typically knows little or nothing about politics and holds positions that may be internally inconsistent and unstable over time, they concede, but collectively all the flaws cancel each other out; through the magic of aggregate statistics, the public as a whole is rational even if nearly all those who constitute it are not. It is therefore a myth that public opinion is fickle. Democracy works because public opinion on issues ranging from social policy to foreign affairs is at the same time relatively constant and capable of change when new circumstances demand it.

Not only are voters reasoning creatures and not only is public opinion stable, but citizens, Morris Fiorina contends, have, and are willing to exercise, the capacity to hold leaders accountable. Again, it is not necessary for voters to carry the *Almanac of American Politics* in their heads to judge the performance of incumbents. In presidential elections, they would be foolish to trust the promises politicians make, but it is within their power to compare what their lives are like now with what they were like four years ago and to act accordingly. Like the rest of us, voters cannot predict the future, but they can hold politicians accountable retrospectively; incumbents who ignore the public's desires, or whose incompetence fails to deliver what voters expect, will be punished the next time an election rolls around. Aware of that possibility, candidates for any office, and not just incumbents, need to be responsive to public concerns.

Such conclusions are meant to assure us that democracy's critics have made too strong a case. Alas, the picture these scholars paint of the state of American democracy is in many ways even more disturbing than the fears of earlier democratic skeptics. Hamilton and Tocqueville were writing before modern democracy came into being and were anticipating what might happen under a worst-case scenario. Today's empirically oriented political scientists, by contrast, are studying what has already happened and are using the best available methodological tools in order to do so. Surely it should matter that much of what they actually have to say raises disturbing questions about how well American democracy performs.

Popkin's concept of low-information rationality, for example, has credibility when a cognitive short-cut can successfully substitute for the larger reality it attempts to represent. That substitution process is often appropriate as voters judge a candidate's character; Al Gore's sighs during his 2000 debates with George W. Bush conveyed relevant signals about the candidate's sense of intellectual superiority. Substitution may also work on issues of domestic policy; George H. W. Bush's surprise at discovering the existence of bar-coded check-out machines in supermarkets effectively symbolized how out of touch with ordinary voters politicians can be. But although Popkin (along with Michael Dimock) tries to make the case that low-information rationality is appropriate for issues of foreign policy, he is, at least to me, unconvincing; a candidate's lack of appreciation for ethnic food conveys no information value whatsoever when it comes to his position on nuclear proliferation.[5] Low-information rationality poses a problem when high information is required, and while high-information topics are often not discussed or are discussed badly during campaigns, they have huge implications for national security and global stability. When it comes to such matters, it is hardly reassuring to learn that Americans have not been lifted up into reason but that criteria of reason have been lowered down to fit their informational shortcomings.

There are similar limits to the notion that the public is

collectively rational whatever the peculiarities of the individuals who compose it. Page and Shapiro work within the tradition of Anthony Downs, one of the first to elaborate upon the implications of "rational ignorance." Assuming that people are utility maximizers, Downs reasoned that they have good grounds not to inform themselves about politics because their votes have little or no effect upon an election's ultimate outcome. This turns out to be anything but a reassuring theory, however. For if all individuals are utility maximizers, elites will have an incentive to monopolize their control over information for the same reason ordinary people will be tempted to remain ignorant; information is a commodity, often a valuable one, and elites will use it to improve their situation relative to those they govern. To their credit, Page and Shapiro recognize this possibility. "The information available to the public may sometimes be overwhelmingly false, misleading or biased," they point out, and under those conditions, "the rational public can be deceived." Democracy cannot necessarily be secured by statistical properties after all.

The beauty of Morris Fiorina's concept of retrospective voting lies in the idea that accountability does not make great demands on citizens; as he puts it, "they need *not* know the precise economic or foreign policies of the incumbent administration in order to see or feel the *results* of those policies."[6] But even the seemingly simple task of comparing one's personal situation now with that of four years ago proves to be complicated. On the one hand, voters barely hold politicians accountable at all. Lacking information about politics, they forget what happened two or three years ago and tend to concentrate on matters affecting their lives only as a new campaign approaches; politicians therefore have a free hand for most of their time in office so long as they try to manipulate the factors that influence public happiness in the run-up to their reelection.[7] On the other hand, voters develop tests of accountability so strict that they lose touch with the real world; politicians actually have little influence on how the economy performs, which means that voters who give them credit or blame in the months before the election are holding them to standards they cannot meet. (This helps explain why voters have a tendency to punish politicians for flu epidemics and shark attacks.)[8] The tendency of voters either to overestimate or to underestimate what politicians are capable of doing is bound to contribute to cynicism so long as people pay little or no attention to what politicians are actually doing.

Information matters. Page and Shapiro write that some forms of information "amount to little more than trivia quizzes" and that not much follows if people fail to know the names of their congressmen or the length of their terms.[9] Yet it would seem fairly obvious, to cite only one example, that Americans are far more likely to support repealing the estate tax if they believe that large numbers of people, including even themselves, will be subject to it rather than the 2.3 percent of Americans who, before the tax was provisionally suspended, actually were.[10] Political scientists such as Martin Gillens and Larry Bartels have gone to great length to demonstrate that lack of information does result in people having views they would not have if they were fully informed.[11] Voting is inevitably cheapened when people do not know for what or for whom they are voting. It may be reassuring to realize that 40 percent of Americans can be induced to offer an opinion on whether the Public Affairs Act of 1975 should be repealed, but it raises serious questions about the existence of an informed public when we learn that there is not, and never was, such a thing as the Public Affairs Act of 1975.[12]

We cannot know what earlier critics of democracy might think if they suddenly materialized among us, had a chance to see democracy in action, and read accounts by political scientists justifying democracy's performance. But it is perhaps safe to conclude that they would find much to confirm their worries. Sometimes the most damning indictment of an institution is offered not by those who condemn it but by those who defend it. Such would appear to be the case with the role of information in democracy in America today. In discussing the low information value of political campaigns, Popkin says that "if campaigns are vulgar, it is because Americans are vulgar."[13] He may be right, but as an argument on behalf of democratic quality, that one is pretty weak. As much as we may want to believe that voters have the factual basis to make informed choices, we may have to face the conclusion that democracy, when it happens, may mostly be a matter of luck.

Americans have been lucky for quite some time. Despite their lack of information about politics, they have done a fairly good job evaluating candidates and the public policies they support. By "good job" I do not mean that Americans wind up agreeing with my own political positions; sometimes they do, and sometimes they do not. Public opinion, rather, much as Page and Shapiro suggest, works to strengthen democracy if it is relatively constant over time (thereby avoiding instability), moderate in expression (thereby skirting extremism), and generally in accord with the views held by elites (thereby reducing cynicism). On many issues of the day, including ones known for their contentiousness, American opinion, even without a strong grounding in fact, has met these criteria.

Consider an issue often presumed to be among the most divisive in American politics. Polls show that Americans tend to be deeply troubled by abortion, yet they also support a woman's right to choose.[14] These views, moreover, are quite stable; from 1972 to the present, there has been no significant shift in the public's attitude toward abortion. Despite much talk about red states and blue states divided by differing moral outlooks on the world, regional differences with respect to abortion are not especially pronounced. (Neither, by the way, are gender differences.) And public opinion on abortion matches fairly closely elite opinion, as reflected in the Supreme Court's attempts to preserve *Roe v. Wade*, even while modifying it, as well as by congressional actions that leave a woman's right to choose in place while restricting forms of abortion that many Americans consider morally problematic. There are political activists determined to make abortion as divisive an issue as they can, yet they have been consistently thwarted by the refusal of most Americans to take up arms in the cause. This reluctance is bound to make you unhappy if you believe that abortion is murder. If, on the other hand, you think that a woman's right to choose should be unrestricted, you will not be comfortable with efforts to moderate *Roe v. Wade*. For nearly everyone else, public opinion works about as well on this issue as a democracy has any right to expect.

Abortion is representative of a whole slew of opinions in which Americans, as if instinctively, reach for the middle position between extremes. On Social Security, the top domestic issue of the first decade of the twenty-first century, they were amenable to new approaches designed to protect the program's fiscal solvency, but, suspicious of privatization, they also wanted to keep the basic concept of insurance intact, while on the war in Iraq, the leading foreign policy issue of the same period, they supported the original invasion but also wanted United Nations approval. So long as politicians take roughly the same position that voters do, congregating toward the center in a search for consensual policies, the public's lack of information is not a significant problem for American democracy. For decades, this is exactly what most politicians did. Anxious to win reelection, determined to secure legislative benefits for their constituents, worried about being characterized by opponents as outside the mainstream, and desperate for funding from established interests with little inclination to rock any boats, politicians worked in bipartisan fashion to maximize pork, sought refuge in the vital center when campaigning, and ran for reelection on the strength of seniority and experience. Such a nonideological style of politics was not especially populistic; moderation was more likely to emerge from bipartisan bargaining inside the beltway than from focus group research inside the district. Still, leaders and followers generally wound up on the same page, and so long as they did, Americans, not knowing that much about politics, could rest assured that politicians would not abuse their ignorance.

No longer. On the issue of abortion, to continue with that example, all the elements that enabled opinion and policy to correspond remain in place *except one:* the accord between what the public thinks and what political elites are prepared to do is breaking down. To reward the religious voters who supported him so strongly, President Bush named two conservative judges, John Roberts and Samuel Alito, to the U.S. Supreme Court. One of them, Alito, filled the seat occupied by Sandra Day O'Connor, who had, during her tenure, refused to overrule *Roe v. Wade.* One can never know what a future Supreme Court will do, but if this more conservative court does opt to overrule *Roe,* as seems at least plausible, the middle-of-the-road position shared by the majority of Americans on this issue will not be the position of the U.S. government. Leaders and followers would not, under such a scenario, be on the same page at all; indeed, they might not even be reading from the same book.

As the example of abortion suggests, whatever one thinks of the programs of contemporary conservatives, no one could charge them with excessive devotion to public opinion. Not only are they willing to run the risk of overturning a Supreme Court decision that is generally popular, many of their legislative initiates are not strongly supported by the public either, including Social Security privatization, limits on stem cell research, and tax cutting that produces significant deficits. They have their agenda; the public has its own; and the public's is the one that will have to give way.

At first glance, this willingness to stand up to public opinion suggests that contemporary conservatives, despite the emergence of the new politics of democracy, are not very populistic after all; they are committed not to what the people want but to what they strongly believe the people should have. Yet first glances in this case are deceiving. For one thing, although Americans know where they stand on an issue such as abortion, they do not hold their views with the passion of the ideologically committed. Not particularly well informed about the actual views of judges nominated to the Supreme Court, they paid relatively little attention to the confirmation hearings of John Roberts and Samuel Alito, trusting that if they were men of integrity, they would put the law first and ideology second. This relative public indifference allows politicians considerable leeway to claim a populist mantle even while taking actions of which the public, in the abstract, might disapprove. The Alito hearings in particular seemed to dispense with the idea that judges opposed to *Roe v. Wade* should mask their opposition lest they arouse an angry public against them.

There are other reasons as well why politicians can claim a populist mantle even while ignoring what the public wants. For ideological politics, even when it cuts against the grain of public opinion, is *semipopulistic* in an informational sense and *hyperpopulistic* in an emotional sense. Ideological politics is semipopulistic in the sense that political elites have perfected the art of rallying those who support them while marginalizing those who do not. And it is hyperpopulistic because those elites, even when proposing policies that stand in opposition to what the public wants, appeal to emotions with which the public resonates.

As if to demonstrate the degree to which both of America's political parties can take advantage of the new politics of democracy, a semipopulistic approach to information shaped the presidency of Bill Clinton. Studying the ways in which Clinton and his advisers tried to build public support for their plan to provide national health insurance, Lawrence Jacobs and Robert Shapiro found that they possessed "low regard for the public's capacity for reasoned and critical thought."[15] In their approach to health care, the Clintons relied on what social psychologists call "priming." Strategies based on priming do not try to win over undecided voters by appealing to facts they may not know. Instead, as Jacobs and Shapiro put it, priming "concentrates on raising the priority and the weight that individuals assign to particular attitudes already stored in their memories." Guided by such an approach, Clinton spent relatively little time trying to persuade the public that he had the details of the policy right while devoting considerable attention to finessing the media, rallying support among favorably inclined interest groups, and searching for what pollster Stanley Greenberg called a "simple core idea" that could "resonate with the public" in order to fend off challenges from Republican opponents.[16] Bill Clinton read polls, not necessarily to follow in the direction they pointed, but to know how to frame his already-chosen programs to be in accord with them. In the old politics of democracy, opinion was the input and policy the outcome. In the new politics of democracy, it is the reverse.

Although bipartisan in origin, priming was brought to fruition by Republicans during the George W. Bush presidency. Whatever the policy, whether the war in Iraq, Social Security privatization, confirmation of judges, or tax cuts, the administration began with a simple but dramatic narrative of crisis: Iraq was a threat to American security, tax cutting would create jobs and stimulate the economy, judges are entitled to up-or-down votes, Social Security would run out of money. Facts were cherry-picked and exaggerated to add credibility to the narrative; in reality, Iraq did not have the weapons the administration claimed; conservatives sank the nomination of Harriet Miers to the U.S. Supreme Court without an up-or-down vote; there is no evidence that supply-side economics works; and Social Security bankruptcy was long down the road, privatization would not stave it off, and moderate reforms would solve the problem, which was in any case a minor potential fiscal crisis compared with looming deficits. Strategy and tactics became a substitute for accurate information about policy proposals. Staying on message became religious in its intensity. The positions of opponents were distorted and caricatured. If a political concept did not sell well in focus groups—"privatization," "the nuclear option"—then other terms—"personal accounts," "constitutional option"—would be found, without, of course, changing the policy. There was little attempt to modify proposals in order to win over swing voters since legislation could pass so long as party discipline remains intact. It was even possible to be up front about one's techniques of manipulation, both to cow the opposition and because so much of the public debate was about tactics rather than substance.

Priming may not always work; it failed President Clinton's health care reform badly and it proved to be of limited effectiveness and perhaps even counterproductive on George Bush's Social Security plans. And even though Mr. Bush won congressional approval for his tax cuts in his first term, rising deficits and pressing needs at home and abroad make it highly unlikely that he will make them permanent in his second. Indeed, Mr. Bush ran into significant and, from his point of view, unexpected difficulties after his reelection. Not only did Social Security privatization collapse, Hurricane Katrina and its aftermath helped put on the political radar screen issues of poverty, which do not play to the strength of the Republican Party, and seriously damaged the president's reputation for competence. As the Jack Abramoff and assorted other corruption scandals engulfed the Republican Party, Mr. Bush found himself in the awkward position of mimicking the tactics of his predecessor, seeking incremental changes in public policy rather than pursuing bold designs to reshape the course of American history. But none of this detracts from the success of priming in President Bush's first term or mitigates against the admittedly hypothetical possibility that such tactics would have continued to work in the second term if the administration had not been so arrogant and politically tone deaf.

As the successful examples of priming demonstrate, when opinion is shaped by policy rather than the other way around, ignorance is no longer just a background assumption in front of which elites struggle for what they want. Instead, ignorance becomes something of value to be cultivated and encouraged, an essential weapon in an effort to shift the public to a place where, if it were better informed, it would not want to go. "Efforts at priming," Jacobs and Shapiro write, "impose less stringent requirements on the public." In using such tools, elites assume that "Americans (and journalists) do not have to acquire and process the kind of extensive information about policy details that a direct persuasion strategy can demand; they need not pay attention to and follow detailed and complex reasoning."[17] Like state governments stripping themselves of regulatory authority in a desperate race to the bottom to encourage industry to locate within their borders, ideologically driven parties outdo each other in their determination to expand the already extensive level of political ignorance in the United States. In such ways is the politics of information semipopulist. Elites do not need widespread public enthusiasm behind their programs in order to see them enacted, as they would in a genuinely populist democracy. Instead, so long as people do not know enough about policies to oppose them, elites can still get what they want. In the best of all possible worlds, elites want the public on their side. In an ideological world, it is sufficient that the public is not on the other side.

At the same time that the new politics of democracy is semipopulistic with respect to information, it is hyperpopulistic in matters of emotion. Unsure about the details of a radically new initiative—whether it comes from the left end or the right end of the spectrum hardly matters, even if these days the most radical proposals come from the right—the public is likely to prefer compromise and moderation, the very dispositions that, for an ideologically committed policy maker, must be avoided. Understanding that public support for radical measures may be lukewarm at best, policy makers prefer to shift the terms of the discussion to emotional issues more likely not only to engage members of the general public but to allow them to identify with the very politicians whose policy proposals they may not like. The public does not seem to mind; indeed it frequently craves more. Uninterested in telecommunications regulation or foreign exchange rates, Americans do not mind hearing tales of brinkmanship, last-minute vote changes of heart, failures of nerve, he-said/she-said squabbles, charges of corruption, and won-lost percentages borrowed directly from sports. The new politics of democracy resembles a daytime television melodrama more than an academic seminar: attention is captured when conscience is tempted, courage displayed, determination rewarded, wills broken, egos checked, pride humbled, and virtue rewarded. In terms of giving the public what it wants, few things can be more satisfying than shifting the discussion from matters of policy to questions of character.

Factual information about politics plays little or no role under conditions of emotional populism. Sincerity, consistency, resolve, determination, conviction—these matter most, even if people are not clear on what their leaders are consistent about or resolved to do. Indeed, actual information about policy may become counterproductive to emotional populism, for factual knowledge can only instill a sense of complication and nuance when politicians seek moral clarity and black-and-white distinctions. If a politician satisfies the public's desire to have a good man in office, it does not matter much what he does. If anything, Americans value emotional identification with leaders so much more than policy positions that they assume—often mistakenly—that any person they admire must share their policy preferences.[18]

Public opinion in the United States has *always* been marked by relatively low levels of information and a preference for emotional identification; the new politics of democracy has changed nothing in that regard. What has changed, however, are the consequences. Although Americans were not harmed by their lack of political information in a more consensual age, their unwillingness to learn about the stuff of policy is likely to harm them considerably in more ideological times. So long as both ordinary people and political leaders converged toward the middle of the spectrum, a person who knew little about politics could nonetheless be fairly sure that any program passed while he was not paying attention would not surprise him after he learned of its details. The system may not have worked elegantly, but work it did.

No sure assurances are available in American politics under the imperatives of the new politics of democracy. As we see in the case of abortion, political information and political intensity, like valuable commodities in general, are unequally distributed. Some Americans have no pronounced views about matters of public policy at all. Others do, but they hold their opinions without much conviction; political scientists who experiment with these sorts of things have discovered how easy it is, by challenging people who express an opinion, to get them to change their views by presenting them with new evidence or arguing against their positions.[19] And even those Americans who do have strong opinions on policy questions generally care about only one or two issues; they know what they believe on gun control but have no idea what they believe, or what candidates believe, on free trade or environmental protection. Whatever attracts Americans to vote and express themselves, it is usually not a desire to see legislation enacted, even on issues that will have major consequences for the lives they lead.

If ordinary Americans care little about policy, however, ideologically driven politicians care greatly—far more so than the more consensually oriented politicians of the recent past.

The major reason to hold office in more ideological times, after all, is not just to provide post offices or highways to the people at home but to put into place new programs that correspond with the preconceived, and very strong, ideas leaders have about how the world ought to be organized. Because elites, in the new politics of democracy, take active advantage of public ignorance and appeal to emotion more than to program, Americans who pay little attention to politics are likely to find that Medicare reform has increased their difficulties in obtaining the medicine they need, tax cutting has raised their taxes, defense spending has lowered their security, and environmental reform has destroyed their favored vacation spot. By then, of course, it will be too late; it is, if not impossible, more difficult to reverse policies when people are paying attention than it is to get them passed in the first place when people are not. In the new politics of democracy, lack of information shifts from being a quirk to constituting a danger. Once relatively cost free, the public's indifference to the basic facts of politics and policy becomes quite expensive, so expensive that Americans frequently fail to recognize how much they are paying.

⁂ One ought never to downplay the importance of emotions in politics; in a democracy, leaders must connect in some satisfying way with the people they plan to lead. But nor should one routinely substitute emotion for policy. So long as politics involves spending taxpayer money on programs that can make the conditions of life of ordinary people easier on the one hand or more onerous on the other, emotional populism may satisfy the public's need for drama, but it can only deepen their alienation from a political system that in theory works on their behalf.

Some political scientists believe that the problems posed by the insufficiency of information are serious but not necessarily

fatal. If we can design techniques to give people more information as they go about developing their views, or if we can
help them understand the consequences of the views they
hold, the performance of democracy can be significantly improved. Such is the reasoning behind the work of one of the
most ambitious and well intentioned of all America's students
of politics, Stanford's James Fishkin.

Fishkin's most important contribution to democracy is
the deliberative poll. Like traditional surveys, deliberative polling selects a randomly chosen group to find out how its members think. But instead of just soliciting answers and then
hanging up the phone, Fishkin and his colleagues, after asking
respondents a series of survey questions, invite them to meet
together for a weekend and offer to pay them for their time and
trouble. In the course of their time together, participants are
given background material and organized into groups presided
over by professional moderators. After two days of intense discussion, individuals are again polled to see whether deliberation changed or deepened their views. Generally, it does both.
Frequently more than half of the participants change their minds
after deliberation. They attribute their change of mind, moreover, to what they have learned through deliberation, which
suggests that their modified views are more informed than
their initial ones. Participants generally indicate an enhanced
intention to vote. Their horizons expand beyond self-interest
to questions of the common good. They are more likely, even
when they disagree on specifics, to agree on the standards by
which policies ought to be evaluated. And they are very likely
to consider the process of deliberation meaningful.

In a political environment characterized by widespread
political ignorance, deliberative polling, according to its supporters, offers a ray of hope. "When the public is given good

reason to pay attention and focus on the issues," Bruce Ackerman and James Fishkin write, "it is more than capable of living up to demanding democratic expectations."[20] To illustrate
the point, they cite the experience of a British deliberative poll
Fishkin conducted dealing with the issue of crime. One par-
ticipant told him that he might as well tear up the question-
naire she had filled out before the experiment because before
her experiences with deliberative polling, she simply did not
know enough about the subject. The spouse of another partic-
ipant told him that she was looking forward to a much more
interesting retirement because now her husband read the newspaper, which he had never done before being asked to join in
the deliberative poll experience. These examples suggest that it
is possible to increase the amount of information citizens have
as they make their political choices. If, as frequently turns out
to be the case, people change their views as they learn more
about the subject under discussion, so much, from the standpoint of democratic functioning, the better.

Fishkin's research demonstrates that people are capable
of acquiring more information about public issues, unques-
tionably good news insofar as the qualitative improvement of
democracy is concerned. But for that very reason, his research
leaves unanswered the question of why Americans so frequently
fail to do so. That question could not be more relevant than it
is under conditions of the new politics of democracy. When
ideologically driven elites are determined to substitute emotion for fact in the hopes of moving opinion in the directions
they favor, the public's incentive to inform itself could not be
greater. Yet at a time when Americans need information more,
they evidently want it even less. The most comprehensive examination of the knowledge Americans have about politics,
which documented a level that by nearly all reasonable stan-

dards was shockingly low, was published in 1996, and there has not been a comparable in-depth study since.[21] Still, the trends are not encouraging: younger Americans, tomorrow's future citizens, are far more likely than their elders to know the winner of *American Idol* or to identify the town in which the Simpsons live, but far less likely to know the party that controls the governorship of their state or the majority in Congress; fewer Americans rely on newspapers to inform themselves of politics in preference to television at a time when television viewers are generally less knowledgeable than newspaper readers; and talk radio and negative campaigning, which overtly tilt information in partisan and ideological ways, are both on the increase.[22] Even if the increased turnout in 2004 turns out to be the start of a new era of political mobilization, newly activated voters during that election were more likely to have cast their ballots based on questions of character than on knowledge of where candidates stood on matters of public policy.

The paradox of needing information more while valuing it less is resolved when viewed as part of a self-fulfilling cycle. Not particularly interested in politics in the first place, Americans feel no incentive to learn more about what is happening in Washington, which only encourages their leaders to take further advantage of their ignorance. When their leaders do exactly that, Americans could respond by blaming themselves for not paying attention and vowing to do better next time. But such introspection is unlikely to be present in a populistic politics committed to praising the common sense of ordinary people. And so Americans typically conclude that they were right to pay so little attention to politics because politicians are so self-interested and manipulative. A cycle in which ignorance breeds blame is therefore fueled by distrust. "The trend since the 1980s of declining government responsiveness to cen-

trist opinion and increased reliance on poll-driven manipulation of public opinion," write Jacobs and Shapiro, "contributed . . . to undermining Americans' confidence in their ability
to influence government and in government itself."[23] Cynical
policies cause cynical politics, and vice versa.

It is not as if Americans suffer a shortage of cynicism to
begin with; the high level of distrust Americans show toward
politics is as well established a finding in political science as is
the low level of information. Seventy-eight percent of Americans trusted government to do what is right just about all or
most of the time in 1964, compared with 29 percent in 1992. (The
figure rose to 44 percent in 2000, still well below the levels of a
generation ago.) In 1964, 69 percent thought that government
was run to the benefit of all, compared with 31 percent who felt
that it was run on behalf of big interests; in 2000 those numbers were almost exactly reversed.[24] The proportion of Americans who trusted government shot up after the attacks on September 11, 2001, but they fell again to their 2000 level as the war
in Iraq continued without success.[25] Younger generations, as it
happens, are more distrustful than older ones, suggesting that
the United States is not about to return soon to a political system that has widespread public support.[26]

Rational voters concerned with policy are likely to turn
cynical when they have great hopes that a favored legislative
proposal will be turned into law and then find themselves disappointed when it is not. But because American voters are neither particularly rational nor especially well informed, their
cynicism raises more serious questions than a mismatch between what they want and what they get. In a rather chilling
analysis, the political scientists John Hibbing and Elizabeth
Theiss-Morse argue that American cynicism is not about policy so much as it expresses unease with the process of democracy itself.

According to Hibbing and Theiss-Morse, Americans believe that the ideal political system should listen to people like
themselves. Alas, they are convinced, government never hears
them; it sells itself to the highest bidder, they believe, giving the
special interests what they ask for rather than giving ordinary
people what they deserve. In reaction, they turn against the
whole process, considering what happens an ugly spectacle
unworthy of their attention. In short, it is not just the policies
political institutions adopt that turn off so many Americans
but also, more important, the way they adopt them. As Hibbing and Theiss-Morse put it, the very things that make democratic politics possible—negotiation and compromise—are
the very things that Americans dislike. "Participation in politics is low because people do not like politics even in the best
of circumstances," they write. "In other words, they simply do
not like the process of openly arriving at decisions in the face
of diverse opinions. They do not like politics when they view
it from afar and they certainly do not like politics when they
participate in it themselves."[27] These are not the kinds of
people one imagines gratefully accepting an invitation to one
of James Fishkin's weekend deliberative polls, but even if they
did, one can hardly imagine them coming home enlightened
from the process.

Some good might nonetheless emerge from this widespread distrust of politics if cynicism led Americans to turn a
watchful eye on their ideologically inclined politicians and to
hold them accountable for their extremism. Yet precisely because their cynicism is tied to process rather than to policy, this
rarely happens. If anything, Americans, for all their distrust of
politics, are surprisingly trustful of politicians. Having given
their support to political leaders because they are impressed
with their character, they are reluctant to withdraw their support when presented with evidence that their leaders may not

be people of strong character after all; Americans were singularly untroubled after they learned that Bill Clinton lied to them while staring them directly in the face (if through television), and although they did eventually come to conclude that George W. Bush was not as honest and trustworthy as they once believed, this was only after Mr. Bush's original justification for the war in Iraq proved to be false and his responses to natural disasters so detached. Hard-boiled on the outside, American political cynicism is squeamishly unformed on the inside. More verbal than it is efficacious, American cynicism is served with heaping portions of naïveté.

Neither cynicism nor naïveté is helpful in highly ideological political periods. The American people are already disposed to dislike the process of democracy because they believe it fails to be responsive to them; one can only wonder how much deeper the national sense of unfairness will become in a more ideological age in which a strong minority is ignored, an indifferent majority is manipulated, and even higher proportions of the federal treasury accrue to the well-off and powerful. One conclusion, though, is already clear, at least if the research of Hibbing and Theiss-Morse is correct: Americans are unlikely to respond either to political extremism or to distortions in the workings of the democratic process by demanding reforms that would restore their faith in democracy. To be sure, Americans do not want their political leaders to lose touch with them. But nor do they want their political leaders to consult with them too much or ask for their input too frequently. They are not especially fond of the new politics of democracy, yet too cynical to imagine that anything would be significantly better, they have resigned themselves to its perpetuation.

If cynicism can be so easily transformed into complacency, naïveté can easily reinforce indifference. Trusting politicians even as they distrust politics, Americans seem frequently unaware that they are no longer governed by people who share their own moderate instincts to avoid contention and controversy but rather by ideological extremists ruthless in their political tactics and determined to bend every rule to their advantage. Intent on reshaping the United States to conform to an ideological vision of the way it should be, America's leaders have knowingly moved into the new politics of democracy. Anxious to retain the luxury of escaping from politics and the demands it places on them, ordinary Americans have not.

Given the tumultuous times through which so many Americans have lived—the 1960s, Vietnam, Watergate, the Clinton impeachment, the 2000 election, September 2001, the Iraqi war, and a potential constitutional crisis over presidential authority during the Bush years—it is perhaps understandable that they learn so little about politics and distrust it so much. America's leaders from both parties have hardly been models of forthright honesty and deeply etched integrity in recent years. Why treat them with respect when they have shown so little respect for those who elect them?

Such reasoning, however, can take one only so far. Ultimately the American public's lack of information about politics stems neither from cognitive limitations hard-wired into the brain, nor from the failure of such institutions as the media to provide them with the information they need, nor from the traumatic experience of having politicians disappoint them. Information gaps exist for one reason only: Americans have the choice to care about politics and have chosen not to. They may think that withholding their support from politicians is a way of punishing them. But it is not; their failure to inform themselves allows their political leaders tremendous leeway to get what they want. Distrust of government constitutes no check on that leeway; if anything, its accompanying naïveté gives politicians even more room to change the world as they see fit.

It is not a pretty sight, this willingness to denounce politicians for their cravenness combined with an unwillingness to pay attention to what they do. When it comes to politics, Americans rely on their cynicism to escape from their obligations, and they trust their naïveté to counter their ignorance. Their views about politics frequently seem more appropriate for spoiled children than for mature adults, as if they want politics to be perfect and, when they discover it is not, they reject it as unworthy. The demands that democracy places upon them are not especially onerous. No one is asking them to devote their lives to politics; all that is required for better democratic performance is that they have some idea what they are talking about and some inclination of where those for whom they vote stand. But these tasks are evidently too demanding for them to take on, and they flock instead to those politicians who appeal to their vanity rather than speak to their needs.

These are harsh conclusions to reach, and they sit uncomfortably with me even as I reach them. One always wants to give ordinary Americans the benefit of the doubt. Frequently there is reason to do so; as I have argued in my own research into American opinion, there is a moderate reasonableness out there in the country, especially on contentious moral issues, that has far more wisdom behind it than the more ideological politics of the activists in Washington.[28] But reasonableness is not enough, not under the conditions of the new politics of democracy. Leaders determined to achieve more ideological outcomes have raised the stakes for Americans, brilliantly taking advantage of their ignorance of and hostility toward politics in ways that can only prey on their fears and destroy their hopes. One can and should blame politicians for this, for they ought to do better, but being politicians, they are likely to take advantage of whatever opportunities present themselves. Ordinary Americans cannot, therefore, avoid their own share of the blame. American democracy will have the quality Americans want. If it is to perform better, they will have to work harder.

III

Democracy Without Accountability

Maybe we expect too much from democracy. The economist Joseph Schumpeter, one of the great modern thinkers to address the question, certainly thought so.[1] Eighteenth-century optimists believed that there was such a thing as the common good, that people could determine it for themselves, and that they would then elect representatives to carry out their will. This "classical theory of democracy," as Schumpeter argued in 1942, was more a quasi-religious expression of hope than an actual description of how democracies worked. There is no such thing as the common good, he delighted in pointing out. And even if there were, ordinary citizens, including the more educated among them, would be too irrational in their desires and too easily fooled to know what it might be. In theory democratic citizens raise and decide issues. In practice, "the issues that shape their fate are normally decided for them."[2]

The primary obligation of citizens, Schumpeter continued, is to produce a government. It is not necessary for them to have in mind some conception of national purpose as they do so. Nor is it essential for leaders to ascertain what is on the minds of voters and to translate those desires into policy. All that is required is that there be a choice between candidates presented to the electorate. Capitalism is an economic system based on competition, and democracy is its political equivalent. Once the electorate installs a government, it need not control it. "Democracy means only that the people have the opportunity of accepting or refusing the men who are to rule them."[3] That's it.

Schumpeter is widely regarded as a hard-headed realist intent on stripping from democracy any trace of romanticism left over from the thought of Jean-Jacques Rousseau. His objective was to identify the rock-bottom requirement that would allow a society to call itself democratic. It is therefore a serious matter that the minimalist one he so identified—competition for political leadership—is on the wane in the United States.

To measure the degree to which competition for political leadership has declined in the United States, it is instructive to consider the recent history of the U.S. House of Representatives. Unlike the Senate, which the authors of the *Federalist Papers* viewed as offering protection against "the impulse of sudden and violent passions," the House would "have an immediate dependence on, and an intrinsic sympathy with, the people."[4] Its members were to be chosen directly by citizens rather than indirectly through state legislatures. Their terms were to be limited to two years. They would be elected in districts whose boundaries would be smaller than the states in which they were located. For all these reasons, the House would be the more democratic of the two legislative branches of the federal government.

Despite these constitutional origins, the U.S. House of Representatives has had more than its share of autocratic leadership. Such powerful speakers of the House as Joseph Cannon (1903–1909) and Sam Rayburn (1940–1946, 1955–1961); long-serving committee chairmen elected from one-party districts and chosen on the basis of seniority; arcane rules mastered by keepers of tradition—all these factors kept power concentrated in the hands of a few. Periods of reform were few and far between, and even when they came about—in response to Watergate, for example, or after 1994 and the Republican "Contract with America"—they tended to be short-lived.[5] If one were searching for models of democratic deliberation and procedure, the U.S. House of Representatives would not be the place to look.

Even when the House was at its most autocratic, however, congressional elections were still relatively competitive; only in the South and in cities such as New York did truly safe seats exist. This is no longer the case. Selection to the U.S. House of Representatives is increasingly organized not by the theory of competitive elections emphasized by Schumpeter but by the reality of what can be called incumbent default. Once you get to the House, almost irrespective of where you came from, your chances of staying there as long as you want have increased dramatically.

Incumbents for any office have built-in advantages over potential challengers to begin with, such as name recognition, the power to support projects beneficial to their districts, and staffs devoted to constituent-pleasing activity.[6] Yet stubbornly persuaded that such advantages did not offer them *enough* protection against potential opponents, members of the House in recent years began to close down the process of who was being elected to it. During the 1970s, for example, the development of political action committees (PACs) gave incumbents significant financial support, especially helpful in an era dominated by rising campaign costs.[7] In the two succeeding decades, incumbency advantage took another giant step forward as parties used their control over state legislatures, as well as the sophistication of new computer programs, to draw electoral districts in ways that ensured continuing party control.[8] Incumbency default is bipartisan business, as applicable to African-American Democrats as it is to Christian right Republicans. However much they may dislike each other, congressmen from both political parties have a shared interest in protecting their seats.

Although incumbency default cannot be attributed to one party or the other, however, it is once again the case that Republicans perfected a technique used more fitfully by Democrats. For surely the ultimate in incumbency protection was achieved when former Speaker Tom DeLay engineered a plan to draw new district lines in Texas favorable to his party without waiting the customary ten years between redistricting efforts; all the eventual gains in Republican seats in the House in the 2004 election could be attributed to DeLay's maneuver. In some states, efforts have been made to reform the redistricting process by taking it out of the hands of self-interested politicians, but those efforts are frequently rejected by voters, as they were, rather resoundingly, in California and Ohio in 2005. The result, as the Democratic political strategist Ed Kilgore has put it, is that politicians are increasingly choosing voters and not the other way around.[9] And since in the first half-decade of the twenty-first century there were more Republican incumbents than Democratic ones, such redistricting efforts will enable more Republicans to pick their own voters than Democrats.

The result of this remarkable determination to protect the seats of those who already hold them is that only a small percentage of elections to the U.S. House of Representatives are contested in any meaningful way. If we define a "safe" seat in the House as one in which the winning candidate receives at least 60 percent of the vote, the decline of the House as a competitive body can be illustrated by the trends presented in Table 1. As this table shows, nearly four out of every five seats in the House are now uncontested.

Incumbency default is not limited to the U.S. House of Representatives but extends to state legislatures and the U.S. Senate.[10] In the 1940s and 1950s, incumbency added only 1 to 2 percent to a candidate's vote; by the 1980s to the 1990s, political scientists estimate, the incumbency advantage had increased to between 8 and 10 percent.[11] One obvious consequence of the fact that incumbents have such significant advantages over potential challengers is that the logic of democracy is turned upside down. The existence of two-party competition is supposed to operate as a check on what incumbents do; potential opposition candidates, intent on taking away the seats of incumbents, will keep a close watch on their votes, publicize any glaring lack of attention to the concerns of ordinary citizens, and raise funds from those disenchanted with incumbents' decisions. In reality incumbents are aware that in the absence of effective competition, no one is paying much attention to how they vote, donors will have little choice but to contribute to them, and they can expect to hold on to their job until they decide to move to higher office, retire in order to cash in from their contacts and experience, or die.

Incumbency default must be acknowledged as one of the most peculiar by-products of the new politics of democracy because Americans are actually not particularly fond of incum-

Table 1. Declining Competition for U.S. House Seats

Election Year	Number of Safe Seats	Safe Seats as % of All Seats
1992	244	56.1
1994	268	61.6
1996	263	60.5
1998	317	72.8
2000	323	74.2
2002	334	76.7
2004	339	77.9

Sources: Michael J. Dubin, *United States Congressional Elections, 1788–1997* (Jefferson, N.C.: McFarland, 1998), 785, 796, 808; John L. Moore, Jon P. Preimesberger, and David R. Tarr, eds., *Congressional Quarterly's Guide to U.S. Elections,* 4th ed., vol. 2 (Wasington, D.C.: CQ Press, 2001), 1218–1227; United States Census Bureau, *Statistical Abstract of the United States, 2004–2005,* 235–248; and "Senate, House, and Gubernatorial Results," *CQ Weekly* 62 (November 6, 2004), 2653–2600.

bents. California voters used the power of the recall to discharge a sitting governor, Gray Davis. In addition, Americans have also lent their support to term limits, which establish a generally low maximum number of times incumbents can run for reelection. Term limits tend to be popular because politicians, especially those already holding office, tend to be unpopular; some 70 percent of Americans say they are "angry" with the federal government, and 60 percent of them explicitly point to Congress as the focus of their discontent, a far greater level of unhappiness than they manifest toward the Supreme Court or the president.[12] True, there exists what political scientists are wont to call "Fenno's paradox": Americans dislike congressmen in general while liking their own in particular.[13] Yet given the low level of knowledge most Americans possess about Congress—the percentage of young Americans who can identify which party controls Congress is actually lower than would be obtained by sheer guesswork—one wonders how deep the support for that person actually can be.[14]

The popularity of recalls and term limits seems to be at radical cross-purposes to the trend toward incumbency default; the last place you want to be when the public gets into one of its angry moods is in a political office from which you can with such dispatch be sent back home. In reality the more populistic features of recent American politics reinforce rather than undermine the protection that politicians have against those who choose them. For one thing, the radical distrust of incumbents manifested in recall elections has much in common with the radical indifference to incumbents witnessed in institutions such as the House of Representatives; in both cases, voters have little knowledge of what causes them either to hate or to admire those who lead them. (This helps explain why California voters, within a year of replacing Gray Davis, began to turn against the candidate they had chosen in his place, Arnold Schwarzenegger, rejecting all the ballot propositions for which the new governor had campaigned.) And by supporting term limits while remaining nonchalant in the face of partisan redistricting, to the point of rejecting efforts to reform the practice, Americans appear to want politicians to evict themselves by rule so that they do not have to dismiss them through the ballot. Term limits and recalls are blunt instruments for controlling what politicians do in highly dramatic situations. But for precisely that reason, they allow politicians that much more leeway to do what they want under more normal conditions without much scrutiny. They are best understood not as mechanisms of political control over politicians but as one more way in which Americans express cynicism toward politics while remaining naïve about politicians.[15]

There is only one surefire way to restore electoral competition in America: the electorate could reassert that protecting this key feature of democracy is in its own hands by voting
against those who benefit from excessive cash or rigged districts. Joseph Schumpeter had little respect for the rationality
of ordinary voters, but he did think that they were capable of
saying no to incumbents from time to time. "In making it the
primary function of the electorate to produce a government,"
he wrote, "I intended to include in this phrase also the function
of evicting it."[16] In the wake of scandals of historic proportion,
voters in the 2006 midterm elections may follow Schumpeter's
advice and evict significant numbers of Republican congressmen from office. (Recall that this book is being written before
those elections take place.) Yet even if Republicans lose seats in
2006, a dramatic shift in the party composition of the House
such as the one that took place in 1994—fifty-four seats shifted
from the Democrats to the Republicans in that year—is highly
unlikely because so many more seats than ever before in American history are safe.

Americans already come out to vote in noticeably small
numbers. When they vote, the knowledge they bring with
them to the polls is minimal. And as if to complete the process
of disaffection from democracy, after they vote they are not
especially interested in keeping tabs on those they elect in
order to decide whether they deserve their continued support.
Eviction, Schumpeter's last-ditch resort, is not generally what
Americans, for all their distrust of politics, think about when
they think about the legislators who represent them; they may
vote some members of Congress out when the institution becomes so corrupt that no one can ignore its scandals, but so
long as business as usual is the rule, the public is not interested

enough in how Congress does its business to insist that all its members face routinely competitive elections before being allowed to sit there.

Competition for political leadership still exists in one corner of American political life: it is impossible to reelect an incumbent when, due to a death or retirement, there is no incumbent to reelect. This appears to be something of a saving grace for democracy; incumbency default decreases competition for reelection, but precisely because safe seats are so valuable to those who hold them, it is likely to increase the competition for open seats in the first place. (An exception must be noted; when a U.S. Senate seat becomes open in midterm, a state's governor can appoint someone to fill the remainder of the term, thereby allowing that person to gain an incumbency advantage without undergoing an initial election.) There will always be fewer initial elections than subsequent reelections, but given that Americans have chosen not to make politics a high priority in their lives, they may feel that democracy is served so long as legislators face intense political competition at least once in their careers.

Yet if Americans pay more attention election than reelection, when it comes to democracy's quality, reelection is far more important than election. The decision to put someone in office, to rely on a distinction made by political philosopher Hannah Pitkin, is a moment of *authorization;* the person we choose is invested with the power to make decisions. Reelections, by contrast, are instances of *accountability;* they acknowledge that our representative has obligations to us as he ponders the decisions he is authorized to make. The difference between authorization and accountability is worth elaborating.

Authorization is generally the focus of democratic minimalists even more skeptical of popular majorities than Joseph Schumpeter; Pitkin cites as the most important Thomas Hobbes, who gives to a strong sovereign virtually unlimited power to do what he wants with the authority invested in him. Accountability theorists, by contrast, are democratic maximalists; by focusing on reelection, they are, as Pitkin puts it, "usually engaged in trying to distinguish 'true' or 'genuine' or 'real' representation from something that has only the outward trappings, that looks like representation but is not." The contrast between authorization and accountability raises a question of form versus substance: are criteria of democracy satisfied so long as the correct procedures are in place, or does democracy require that ordinary voters exercise real control over those for whom they vote? By focusing on a candidate's initial election to office while all but ignoring what their representatives do after they are elected, Americans are opting for an authorizing conception of democracy rather than one based on accountability.

Authorization fits the mood of the new politics of democracy better than accountability because it does not require close attention to what office holders are doing. Given their alienation from politics, Americans generally believe that it is up to Congress to find ways to represent the American people, not up to the American people to hold Congress accountable for its actions. Accountability, in that sense, has not disappeared; if a congressman were to bluntly inform his constituents that he is under no obligation to take their views into consideration, he would probably be voted out of office. But accountability has been seriously weakened. Pitkin writes that unlike authorization theorists, those who stress accountability place importance on "genuine free elections, a real choice of candidates, [and] free communications."[17] These, however, are precisely the features of electoral campaigns that are becoming rarer with the emergence of the new politics of democracy. Accountability is increasingly something of a last resort, appropriate under extreme conditions, but not to be wielded too often and too aggressively.

What happens to democratic institutions when little real accountability exists among those chosen to sit in them? It should not be surprising to learn they lose much of the democratic character by which they carry out their internal affairs. No better illustration of this outcome can be found than the House of Representatives itself. As incumbency default increasingly characterizes the way its members are chosen, the House has put behind it the reformist zeal once associated with both parties and has begun to resemble the more autocratic institution of earlier times.

Any political party will try to use its control over a legislative body to advance its interests; Democrats were certainly no strangers to manipulating the rules to their own benefit when they controlled Congress. But nothing in recent American history resembles the extent to which Republicans relied upon the majorities they gained between 2000 and 2006 to curtail the influence of the minority party. The rules fashioned in Congress by the Republican majority during this period were epitomized by the decision of Speaker of the House Dennis Hastert not to move legislation that has majority support in the House unless it also has the support of a majority of Republicans. Such a practice replaced negotiation and compromise with the kind of politics more associated with one-party states than two-party systems of electoral competition.

One example involves decisions on how much debate will be permitted on proposed legislation in the House of Representatives. House procedures permit either the application of an "open" rule, which allows for amendments, or "restrictive" or "closed" rules, which allow few or no amendments; in the 104th Congress (1995–1996), 45 percent of the legislation was considered under open rules, compared with 22 percent in the 108th Congress (2003–2004; see Table 2). These figures, compiled by a Democrat, Rep. Louise Slaughter, have been challenged by Republicans, who classify restrictive rules as open, but even if we include only the number of closed rules, about which there is no dispute, their number more than doubled in the same period.

The lack of democratic deliberation in the House can also be measured in other ways. The House typically devotes two days a week to suspending the rules so that noncontroversial legislation, such as the naming of post offices, can pass quickly. By adding another suspension day, the House reduced the number of days it is in session to carry out serious legislative business; in the 1980s the House would be in business roughly 280 or 290 days a year, but as Table 3 suggests, that number has been decreasing over the past decade. One result is that the amount of House business conducted under suspension of the rules has increased, as if it were somehow appropriate for more and more time to be spent on issues of less and less importance. Anyone sitting in the House gallery expecting to see something resembling a deliberative body weighing matters of state will be disappointed.

Congress, of course, is still called upon to pass important, and therefore controversial, legislation, such as a prescription drug package, an energy bill, or a law responding to the recommendations of the September 11 commission, but when it does so, the number of hours permitted for debate on these issues has been laughably small, as a glance at Table 3 indicates; it would be difficult to claim that democracy is oper-

Table 2. Democratic Deliberation,
House of Representatives

Congress	% of Open Rules	% of Closed Rules	Days in Session	Bills Considered Under Suspension
104th (1995–1996)	44	19	289	401
105th (1997–1998)	36	24	248	617
106th (1999–2000)	37	39	272	893
107th (2001–2002)	28	23	265	685
108th (2003–2004)	22	36	243	920

Sources: "Broken Promises: The Death of Deliberative Democracy," compiled by Rep. Louise M. Slaughter (2005), 13, 15; telephone interview, minority staff, Rules Committee, U.S. House of Representatives, March 15, 2005; Congressional Research Service, "Suspension of Rules in the House: Measure Sponsorship by Party," January 6, 2005, http://www.house.gov/rules/97-901.pdf.

ating at its best when House members are given forty seconds to read each page of the conference report dealing with the taxation of dividends or twenty seconds per page to read the Department of Defense budget authorization for fiscal year 2004. Nor is democracy served when the minority party is excluded from having a say in the legislation passed by the House; in the 108th Congress no amendments from Democrats were permitted on the Medical Malpractice Reform Act, the Dividend Tax Reduction Act, or the Energy Policy Act. Indeed, the list of procedures adopted by the Republican leadership to exclude the minority party from participation in policy is a long one: forming conference committees to reconcile bills with the Senate without members of the opposition party; closing down committee hearings to prevent Democrats from asking questions at them; and ignoring rules holding votes open for five minutes in order to ensure that bills they support

Table 3. Rushed Legislation, 108th Congress (2003–2004)

Conference Report	# of Printed Pages	Hours Allowed to Read
Omnibus Appropriations FY03	1,507	12
Dividend Tax	299	3¾
FY04 Defense Appropriation	898	5
Energy Bill	571	10
Prescription Drugs/Medicare	852	20
Omnibus Appropriations FY04	1,186	6½
FSC/ETI Tax Package	821	6¼
FY05 Defense Appropriation	938	25½
Omnibus Appropriations FY05	1,645	7
9/11 Commission Recommendations	244	4

Source: "Broken Promises: The Death of Deliberative Democracy," compiled by Rep. Louise Slaughter (2005).

muster enough votes to pass. Congresswoman Slaughter, whose office has documented so many of these trends, describes the floor of the House as a "democracy-free zone," an extreme-sounding statement but one that seems justifiable given the way the U.S. House of Representatives is currently conducting its affairs.[18]

It is not necessarily true that safe electoral districts will produce highly ideological politicians; low turnout in primary elections may be more responsible than redistricting for ideological polarization in the House. But by definition safe seats do produce leaders who, because they need not worry much about electoral challenges, can govern as if their party, and only their party, is the one that matters. When studying an institution with as long and as colorful a history as the U.S. House of Representatives, we may be tempted to conclude that,

whatever the current abuse uncovered or shocking practice exposed, it is all just business as usual. It is therefore sobering
that two such careful and relatively nonpartisan observers of
Congress as Norman Ornstein and Thomas E. Mann can conclude that the way Republicans have recently used their power
in the House is unprecedented. "Over the past five years," they
conclude, "the rules and norms that govern congressional deliberation, debate, and voting—what legislative aficionados
call 'the regular order'—have routinely been violated, especially in the House of Representatives, and in ways that mark
a dramatic break from custom."[19] Sometimes there really are
new things under the sun, and both the degree of incumbency
protection and the movement away from procedures that permit the minority party to hold the majority party accountable
for its actions are among them.

Common sense suggests that office holders facing decreasing
competition in their districts and less need to compromise
with the other party once in office will have a freer hand to vote
as they think best and not as the public thinks best. Yet in this
case, common sense, while not quite wrong, does not convey
the true costs to the quality of American democracy that follow from the way institutions such as the U.S. House of Representatives elect their members and carry out their business.

One of the most important qualities political institutions
in a democracy should possess, we are frequently told, is responsiveness to public opinion. "Democracy," the political scientist Sidney Verba has written in this regard, "implies responsiveness by governing elites to the needs and preferences of the
citizenry. More than that, it implies equal responsiveness; in
the democratic ideal, elected officials should give equal consideration to the needs and preferences of all citizens." If we focus

on political participation, Verba points out, the criterion of equality is rarely met; people with sufficient resources nearly always participate more than those who lack them. Fortunately for democracy, public opinion polling can offer what participation cannot. "Surveys produce just what democracy is supposed to produce—equal representation for all citizens. The sample survey is rigorously egalitarian; it is designed so that each citizen has an equal chance to participate and an equal voice in participating."[20]

Some evidence does exist to suggest that under the rules of the new politics of democracy, America's political institutions are becoming less responsive in the way Verba uses that term. The political scientist Alan Monroe, for example, found that the decisions made by federal officials were in correspondence with public opinion 63 percent of the time in the years between 1960 and 1979, compared with 55 percent of the time between 1981 and 1993; only in the area of national defense was there greater agreement between public opinion and public policy in the later period, while on issues involving welfare, economics, foreign policy, and political reform, significant gaps emerged.[21] No comparable in-depth studies exist for the years that follow, but one tentatively found declining policy responsiveness during the Clinton years on issues involving welfare, crime, social security, and health care, and another discovered especially significant disparities between public opinion and policy on the part of Republican members of the House in the early 1990s.[22] Reviewing these data, Lawrence Jacobs and Robert Shapiro write that "the practice of American government is drifting from the norms of democratic responsiveness."[23]

Still, fears of declining responsiveness do not tell the whole story. Responsiveness, for one thing, is not always good.

Sometimes politicians need to take unpopular actions, such as Lyndon Johnson's decision to support a civil rights law that would doom his party's chances for success in the South; politicians who ignore public opinion to do what is moral, or in the long-term interests of the public, or necessary to resolve a contradiction in public opinion, are strengthening democracy rather than weakening it. Being unresponsive to dangerous opinion is a more valuable political virtue that being responsive to it.

More important, responsiveness and accountability are not the same thing. Responsiveness, as its name implies, has mechanical properties; we say that an automobile engine is responsive if it starts immediately when the ignition key is turned. Aristotle once famously said that man is a political animal; by that criterion, responsiveness is not especially political because it can be satisfied in the absence of significant human activity: in a perfectly responsive universe, machines could measure exactly what Americans believed and then instruct legislators how to vote, all the while ignoring the actual stuff of politics, such as uncertainty, bargaining, and compromise.

In contrast to responsibility, accountability, as *its* name implies, involves telling a story. Storytelling is a quintessentially human activity; we would never say that a car is accountable to the person who starts it, but we would say that someone who is starting the car in order to go to work can give an account of his intentions. Because it possesses a human dimension, accountability requires some form of active, and most likely interactive, communication between office holders and those they represent. We need not, for the sake of accountability, go all the way to the deliberative democracy weekends organized by James Fishkin. But it is important, if democracy is to be called accountable, not only that voters and leaders talk to each other, but that they talk in ways that enable them to explain their positions to each other. There exists, let it be acknowledged, huge amounts of talk in American politics: the airwaves are filled with talking heads analyzing political events; politicians spend fantastic sums on advertising, at least some of which convey information; book publishers issue an uncountable number of screeds, resembling in their own way the pamphlets of the Revolutionary and Jacksonian periods, in which conservatives denounce liberals and vice versa. And yet for all the voluminous talk that characterizes contemporary American politics, neither the way office holders talk to the electorate nor the way the electorate talks back to them attaches much significance to the credible explanation of actions.

The talk preferred by office holders in the new politics of democracy, as Jacobs and Shapiro argue, is increasingly "crafted," as the authors designate all those efforts to find the appropriate language to make already-decided-upon policy proposals seem more in accord with public opinion than they actually are. For Jacobs and Shapiro, this reliance on crafted talk makes democracy less responsive, but the real danger is that it makes democracy less accountable. Indeed, crafted talk is deliberately designed to be antiaccountable. Partisan and ideological in origin, crafted talk does not provide politicians with an opportunity to explain what they are doing; its entire rationale is to obfuscate what policy makers intend to do, as if the only purpose of even contemplating an explanation of what a policy maker has in mind is to ward off potential objections should others actually perceive his intentions. If crafted talk is the norm, then the more debates, advertising, and media talk shows America has, the less accountable its democracy becomes.

Although there has been considerable discussion of the inauthentic ways in which leaders talk to followers, it is also

important to focus on the way ordinary Americans share responsibility for the low level of explanation in American politics. Americans feel no particular need to explain themselves
to their leaders because, in their minds, politics ought to be a
self-explanatory affair. As John Hibbing and Elizabeth Theiss-
Morse point out, Americans believe that everyone knows, or
ought to know, what is right and just: affordable health care,
economic growth, a strong national defense, good education,
low crime rates, a balanced budget. (Just as they attribute their
own beliefs to the politicians for whom they vote, Americans
also attribute to the majority the views they personally hold.)[24]
They see no reason to explain why these are good things; common sense simply makes clear that they are, and politicians
should stop all the posturing and bickering and just see that
these goods are accomplished. Yet to the perpetual dismay of
large numbers of Americans, this is exactly what politicians
never seem to do. Rather than responding by sharpening their
attention to politics and demanding action in favor of what
they believe, Americans typically withdraw even farther from
active political engagement when politicians, as they see it, so
repeatedly fail to do what they should.

The ability of ordinary Americans to talk in ways that
would hold politicians accountable to them is further com-
promised by the fact that their demands frequently contradict
one another. To cite the most obvious case, Americans want
their leaders to add an ever-expanding number of benefits to
those they already have, even while believing that it is possible
to shrink the size of government; one difficulty with the idea
that politicians should be responsive to public opinion is that
if they really were, they would find themselves tied up in knots.
Taking accountability seriously means asking Americans to be
more introspective, even self-critical of their expectations; but,

reluctant to challenge their own assumptions, and in any case constantly flattered by those who seek their votes, ordinary Americans attribute whatever faults their democracy possesses not to themselves but to those who govern them. Weak conceptions of accountability in that sense let Americans off the hook. They can continue to believe that there are no hard choices in politics, and that politicians who think otherwise are just lazy and incompetent, without having their illusions shattered.

One might think politicians, wanting to be admired by those who choose them, would demand a more consistent set of instructions to follow and would appreciate less hostility toward the kind of work they do. But on the contrary, most of them understand, as most of the electorate does not, that both ignorance of and hostility toward politics, by removing accountability from the hands of ordinary people, removes it from the duties of politicians as well. Politicians seeking a relatively free hand to get what they want, especially if what they want is unpopular or has no mandate, prefer a political system characterized by suspicion and withdrawal to one united by any sense of common national purpose. In this sense, the not very democratic—but at the same time very partisan and divisive—U.S. House of Representatives is the perfect symbol of the way politics is carried out in a democracy in which strong forms of accountability do not exist.

The new politics of democracy is built upon a great divide between left and right. But just as important is the gap between people and politics. We have a world of political participation, voting, and opinion surveying in which people tell politicians what is on their minds, and we have a world of policy making, strategizing, and campaigning in which politicians, when not attacking each other, appeal for public support—and neither has much to do with the other. Unwilling to cross the divide, the electorate gets angry because it feels slighted. Eager to perpetuate the divide, office holders become arrogant toward those they so easily manipulate. When the two meet—as they inevitably do during elections, or when the attention of the public is grabbed by an especially controversial policy proposal—they approach each other warily, as if people would be a lot better off without politics and politicians much better off without people. Because they can never avoid each other completely, there will always be some accountability, the one to the other. But because of their mutual contempt, accountability in America is haphazard, indirect, and incomplete. Joseph Schumpeter's great fear was that democratic theorists suffered from an excess of idealism. Under the new politics of democracy, both citizens and leaders possess far too much cynicism.

For all of its flaws, the new politics of democracy can still hold politicians accountable for what they say and do. Lest anyone doubt this, a striking example was offered during the 2005 debate over President Bush's plan to privatize aspects of the Social Security system. This political struggle started, as do so many in contemporary American politics, with crafted talk; the president proclaimed a crisis, selectively chose the facts to back up his claims, and engaged in efforts to divide the electorate by self-interest. Political insiders in both the president's camp and in the ranks of the Democratic opposition were perfectly aware that the president's objective was not to ensure the fiscal solvency of Social Security; Social Security was a stand-in for a debate over the legacy of the New Deal, involving nothing less than the question of whether the United States should adopt a new public philosophy to replace one that had been in existence for seventy years. Yet even though President Bush acknowledged that privatization would not solve Social Security's threatened insolvency, the radical nature of his plan, at least at first, did not receive much attention. In a political system characterized by weak conceptions of accountability, opponents of Social Security could, and did, claim that they were merely trying to reform the system—indeed to save it in ways of which Democrats such as the late Daniel Patrick Moynihan would have approved—rather than to abolish its key guarantees of inviolable retirement benefits.

Certainly to President Bush's surprise, and perhaps to the surprise of his Democratic opponents as well, crafted talk, scare tactics, and partisan base rallying simply did not work. Americans generally liked Social Security and did not want to see it changed; in classic democratic fashion, they let their leaders know, in no uncertain terms, where they stood. When it comes to a program as reliable and universal as Social Security, Americans possess a strikingly accurate amount of knowledge about how the system works, understand and can explain its basic public purpose, and can be quite active in rallying to its support. Social Security privatization, for the moment, has been dropped from the Republican agenda, and given the unpopularity of the idea, it may never return. The whole episode shows that in the new politics of democracy, weak conceptions of accountability do not imply the absence of any accountability at all.

At the same time, however, programs and policies that are new, unfamiliar, and more distant from the concerns of the majority of Americans are subject to significant distortion because of the inability to hold politicians accountable for their actions. Here the relevant example is the war in Iraq. The tactics deployed to build support for the war were identical to those that would later be used to try to weaken Social Security: the proclamation of a crisis, a reliance on distorted information meant to confuse the public, and the application of partisanship so extreme as to call into question the loyalty of those who questioned the policy. But unlike what happened with Social Security, crafted talk and the tactics that go with it worked well politically in the case of Iraq; President Bush was able to win congressional support for his actions, and before long American troops found themselves fighting in a distant part of the world.

The war in Iraq would eventually prove as unpopular as Social Security privatization, but George W. Bush never paid a political price; voter unhappiness with the war did not surface to any significant degree until after the president was reelected in 2004. (As it happens, none of the unelected officials who planned and executed the war, such as Secretary of Defense Donald Rumsfeld, paid much of a price either, given President Bush's reluctance to hold them accountable for their frequently incompetent decisions.) Of course Mr. Bush's party may someday be held accountable if victory is not achieved and American causalities continue to mount, although Republican leaders, fully aware of that possibility, are likely to find themselves engaged in efforts to draw down the number of troops in Iraq before long. Whatever the future holds, however, democratic accountability has not worked well in this war; Americans were too shaken by the events of September 11 to challenge the rationale for the invasion of Iraq, too committed to unity when Americans were dying to have had a full debate about the war, and too reluctant to change leadership during war to vote out of office the man responsible for launching it.

The war in Iraq, moreover, was viewed by President Bush as a key battle in a larger war against terrorism. As if aware that

Americans were not assigning high importance to political accountability—how could they be if they were willing to watch vibrant democracy all but disappear from the U.S. House of Representatives?—Mr. Bush launched one of the most sustained attacks on the idea of accountability in American history. "Well, we had an accountability moment, and that's called the 2004 election," the president told a group of reporters from the *Washington Post* in January 2005.[25] Once that moment had passed, it became clear that the president believed himself unbeholden to the other branches of government. Although Congress had passed the Foreign Intelligence Surveillance Act in 1978, and although the courts established by that act had overwhelmingly approved executive-branch requests for electronic surveillance, President Bush not only authorized such acts without consulting the FISA courts, he claimed justification for his actions by citing a decision of Congress to authorize force in Afghanistan, a claim that even members of his own party in Congress did not take seriously. It is possible that Congress will try to reestablish its authority over unauthorized wiretaps in one way or another. Yet even if it does, Americans have to accept the fact that they duly elected a president whose conception of his office left little room for such basic democratic requirements as public scrutiny and debate.

With respect to accountability under the new politics of democracy, then, the news is mixed. It is good news that when Americans care enough, they can both explain to politicians why a program like Social Security matters to them and demand straight answers from their leaders even when the latter are not disposed to provide them. But it is not good news that their lack of interest in and attention to politics increasingly results in the election of leaders who put accountability to such frequent and strenuous tests, as President Bush has done.

There may be no more important question facing the future of American democracy than this one: will the politics around Social Security or the politics around the war on terror become the model for future discussion and policy making? If the former, there is hope for accountability in the new politics of democracy. But if the political dynamic around the war on terror is repeated, authorization rather than accountability will be the order of the day. It does not bode well in this context that President Bush envisions the war on terror as a long-term struggle, for this suggests that so long as someone, somewhere, plans to attack Americans, accountability will apply only during elections and not between them. By putting such an emphasis on authorization rather than accountability, Mr. Bush has indicated the degree to which his understanding of politics has been shaped not by Thomas Jefferson and James Madison but by Niccolò Machiavelli and Thomas Hobbes.

Americans, of course, are free to reject a conception of accountability so alien to their history and traditions. For them to do so, however, they will need to pay far more attention, not only to the powers that presidents claim, but to the practices that politicians at all levels of government engage in. Unlike construction projects and highways, accountability is a political good that cannot be offered by those in power, whatever their political party or ideological stance on the world. It exists only if ordinary voters insist upon it. Democracy has this one great advantage: it permits Americans to do more than authorize their leaders to act; it allows them to hold their leaders accountable for their actions. It also has this one great challenge: whether or not Americans demand such accountability is up to them.

IV
Democracy Without Institutions

No definition of democracy has better stood the test of time than Abraham Lincoln's "government of the people, by the people, for the people." However inspiring an ideal, however, Lincoln's characterization has always been inaccurate as fact. Throughout most of U.S. history, people did not organize the government and the government did not respond to people. Between the one and the other stood institutions: political parties, the press, business organizations and trade associations, labor unions, churches, lobbyists, reform associations, fraternal and social groups—in short, the entire panoply of voluntary associations that has drawn the attention of acute observers from Alexis de Tocqueville to Robert Putnam.[1] A society in which power flows to the top is too authoritarian, a society in which authority seeps down to the bottom too anarchistic, to be democratic. Democratic life is institutional life.

Institutions may be a requirement of democracy, but democracy makes their preservation difficult. Americans have a deep love of freedom, so deep that it frequently resists the first requirement of institutional life: the need to join with others to realize collectively goals that cannot be achieved by individuals alone. Only this pervasive individualism explains why so many Americans attend churches that have severed ties from denominations, resist belonging to labor unions no matter how insecure their jobs or low their incomes, or move so frequently that they lack strong ties to any particular community.[2] Whether Tocqueville was right for his time is a question for historians to debate; were he to visit today, he might well be as impressed by the anti-institutional features of American culture as by the vibrancy of voluntarism.

The anti-institutional instincts of Americans are linked to their populist sensibilities; distrustful of politics, they not surprisingly also view with suspicion the institutions that make politics possible. Yet such skepticism is misplaced: democracy works best in a dense ecology of political institutions capable of aggregating individual voices, representing different interests, developing sufficient power to check the prerogatives of one another, and forging coalitions that make majority rule possible. In the new politics of democracy, many of America's most important political institutions, such as political parties and interest groups, have found themselves challenged by increasing skepticism from below and a more ideological and partisan atmosphere from above. Thus is added one more arena in which the populist inclinations of Americans, ultrademocratic on the surface, work against what is required for effective democratic governance.

Political partisanship is strikingly strong in the United States these days. Political parties are unusually weak. Between these seemingly contradictory developments lies a story with important implications for American democracy.

Parties stand so clearly in first place in the rankings of political institutions that without them, many political commentators insist, democracy as we understand it would be impossible. Parties perform a nearly uncountable number of functions for democracy, including collating opinion into relatively coherent form, selecting candidates to run for office, mobilizing support for them once they do, organizing the work of the legislative bodies to which they are elected, and providing for continuity between one era and the next. It is true that America's founders failed to anticipate parties. But it is equally true that institutions that developed in the absence of planning are all the stronger, their rationale dependent not on constitutional rules but on actual performance.

Despite their importance, political parties are being transformed in the new politics of democracy. And the reason, as in so many other areas of American political life, is that political parties could not hold themselves aloof from the democratizing movements so visible in the United States in the aftermath of the 1960s.

Among Democrats, attempts to work around the influence of political parties could be detected long before the 1960s; as Sidney M. Milkis has demonstrated, twentieth-century liberals, none more so than Franklin Delano Roosevelt, preferred a political system in which the federal bureaucracy would do much of the work of organizing rewards and winning allegiances that parties once did.[3] But those trends were severely exacerbated as a new generation of political activists came on the scene thirty years later, determined to put into practice notions of participatory democracy they inherited from their days as student protestors. Even before he became a (losing) presidential candidate, George McGovern presided over reforms that broadened participation within the Democratic

Party and, by doing so, weakened the ability of the Democrats to act as a political party in the traditional sense; more power to primary voters meant less power for those who assembled behind proverbial closed doors to choose nominees. For more than a century, the Democratic Party contained both machine-type professionals comfortable in smoke-filled rooms and reformist-inclined amateurs determined to give ordinary voters a greater say in the party's affairs. Eventually the battle for the soul of the party was won by the latter.

The Republicans may be the more conservative party, but they too attracted their movement activists, many of whom, such as Karl Rove, Grover Norquist, Jack Abramoff, and Ralph Reed, rose to power through Young Republican clubs on campuses across the country. Grassroots conservatives had distrusted the East Coast wing of their party since at least 1952, when their preferred candidate, Robert A. Taft, was passed over in favor of General Eisenhower, an uncertain Republican at best. Since then conservatives, like liberal reformers within the Democratic Party, have relied on activists in the party's base, especially in party primaries, to nominate Republican candidates for president with strong ties to organizations that, while allied with the Republican Party, are not officially part of the party apparatus.[4] (In various ways and at various times, the Moral Majority, the Christian Coalition, and even such explicitly religious groups as the Southern Baptist Convention have played this role.) In the one party as in the other, party political professionals still exist, but they no longer call the shots as candidates rely on amateur foot soldiers eager to join the cause.

As party professionals lost many of their core functions, especially the ability to choose nominees and to finance and organize their campaigns, political scientists in the 1980s began to talk about the decline of party government in the United

States. Considerable evidence existed to back up their claim. The number of people who strongly identified with one party or the other fell from 75 percent in 1952 to 63 percent in 1988.[5] Ticket splitting, almost unheard of when political parties were stronger, came close to doubling over the same period.[6] By the late 1980s, more Americans identified themselves as independents than as either Democrats or Republicans.[7] No wonder that Walter Dean Burnham could speak of the "dissolution of the parties as action intermediaries in electoral choice and other politically relevant acts," and Gerald Pomper could warn of "a free-floating politics, in which prediction is hazardous, continuities are absent, and governmental responsibility is impossible to fix."[8]

In place of party-centered politics, the story continues, there emerged a "candidate-centered" era in American politics. "The change in focus from parties to candidates is an important historical trend, which has gradually been taking place over the last several decades," the political scientist Martin Wattenberg wrote in 1991.[9] Wattenberg's remarks were prompted by the success of Ronald Reagan, a Republican who had been something of an insurgent against his party and whose popularity was due to such personal qualities as reliability and charisma, not to his (often polarizing) ideology. In a candidate-centered political universe, office seekers make their own decision to run, put together a personal fund-raising team or rely on their personal fortunes, depend heavily on television and other media, win as many contested primaries as they can, are crowned with great fanfare by their nominating conventions, accept federal funds in return for curtailing party support, run rhetorically against Washington, and spend relatively little of their political capital building up party organizations, especially if doing so would compete with their own political ambitions. Although

Wattenberg wrote primarily about Reagan, his analysis applies equally well to some of his successors, such as Bill Clinton, another relative outsider who, in his much criticized strategy of "triangulation," positioned himself halfway between the Republicans and more liberal elements in his own political party.

Lately, many political scientists have concluded that the idea of candidate-centered politics can be taken too far. Parties have not disappeared as politics becomes more candidate centered, they point out, but have instead adapted and flourished in this new atmosphere. Despite the prevalence of soft money, parties continue to be important fund-raising institutions. National parties play an active role in recruiting candidates for office, both to Congress and in the states, and they help state and local parties turn out the vote.[10] It comes as no surprise to those who think this way that talk of party decline during the 1980s actually foreshadowed what would become obvious in the 1990s: a shift in the electorate away from the one party toward the other. Not only did the Republicans sweep the 1994 midterm congressional elections, but the percentage of the electorate that identified with the Democrats in that year was the smallest in recent history, while the percentage identifying with the Republicans was the largest.[11] Once it had become clear that the parties were realigning rather than dealigning, split-ticket voting decreased and partisan voting increased, all suggesting that Americans were not about to give up on their political parties at any time soon.[12]

Skeptics of party decline were right to insist that the emergence of a candidate-centered form of politics did not foreclose important roles for parties to play. Still, there is no doubting that today's parties no longer resemble the ones associated with an era in which strong institutions were accepted as inevitable. One of the political scientists resistant to the idea of party decline, John Bibby, writes that despite the new role that parties are playing in a candidate-centered system of politics, they nonetheless "bear scant resemblance to either the old-style organization of the late nineteenth century or the organizations that existed in the 1950s and 1960s."[13] He is correct, and the differences between parties today and those of the not too distant past have important implications for the new politics of democracy.

Older-style parties were primarily instruments of mobilization. Especially among the urban political machines, but also true more generally elsewhere, parties got out the vote by offering face-to-face contact, simplifying messages to help people with the bewildering complexities of politics, and relying on other strong institutions, such as ethnic associations, labor unions, and fraternities. Mobilization required effective organization, not ideological commitment. The objective was to fashion a majority, and this could be done only by drawing divergent kinds of people together into coalitions united not by a common stance on the issues of the day but by the rewards that would follow from being a member of a winning team. True, those rewards were frequently material in nature—contracts, construction projects, jobs—and the politics of mobilization often became the politics of corruption. Oddly, however, people did not seem to mind; voting, as well as support for political institutions, was higher before reformers cleaned up politics than it has been in our decidedly less corrupt modern era.

Political parties today, to rely on a distinction made by the political scientist Steven Schier, are instruments of activation rather than of mobilization.[14] Activation works from the top down rather than from the bottom up. Office holders, the interest groups that support them, and the ideological activists who identify with them recognize that the general public is not nearly as partisan as they are. Their aim is not to mobilize in general but to target in particular. More sophisticated polling techniques, focus groups, and the wonders of direct mail replace the carpooling and phone calling of the past. The ideal activation campaign is inwardly self-reinforcing rather than outwardly expanding; ideologically motivated partisans financed by supportive interests appeal through their own network of cable television stations and newspapers to core contributors and voters. Democrats and Republicans have both relied on activation strategies; Howard Dean's campaign for the Democratic presidential nomination in 2004 used Internet technology and student volunteers to rally a precommitted base. Primary campaigns, however, generally seek to activate the base, and for that reason there was nothing especially unusual about Dean's strategy. Compared with Dean's strategy within his own party, Karl Rove's reliance on activation rather than mobilization in the 2004 general election was a greater gamble and a more radical break with tradition. Conventional political wisdom, based on principles of motivation, held that candidates should moderate their messages in order to bring out unpersuaded voters in the ideological center. Rove, in contrast, proved that a candidate could be elected by activating ever-greater numbers of core voters in the party's base.

It was, in short, not just the Republican Party that won in 2004 but a new way of thinking about the role political parties should play in a democracy. Activation does not require the same kind of well-organized political parties that mobilization did; hollowed-out party organizations, which are primarily transmission belts for receiving funds from one group and sending them out to others, are sufficient for the task. Nor does activation assemble large groups into majorities; on the contrary, the science of activation is premised upon breaking down the electorate into as many definable subgroups as possible and trying to appeal to each one on the basis of the single issue that appeals to it. There are times, paradoxical as it may sound, when activation requires demobilization, either by suppressing voters generally (for example, through negative advertising) or by seeking to discourage voting among groups likely to favor one's opponent. In the era of mobilization, parties were strong in local communities and relatively weak in Washington; today, their Washington offices are growing even as on the local level they are supplanted by the importance of media-saturated campaigns. Activation is expensive, and parties are required to raise the funds to support it, but those funds are spent not on activities that make parties stronger but on media advertising. The role of parties in an era of activation supplements rather than replaces a candidate-centered political universe; candidates still by and large recruit themselves, depend on their own networks for funds, and remain more loyal to the causes that motivate them than to the party that supports them.

Activation has dramatically changed both the tone and the practices of American democracy. When mobilization was in flower, the Democratic Party contained liberals and southern conservatives, just as within the Republican Party there were northeastern moderates and western conservatives, but in more ideological times, one party tends to stand one way on an issue such as abortion and the other the other way. Not only are the parties more ideologically coherent, moreover, but each party tends to be dominated by its own ideological extreme, resulting in fewer office holders from either party who can be considered political moderates. The consequences are striking; according to the research of Keith Poole and Howard Rosenthal, only 8 percent of House members were centrists in

2004, compared with 33 percent in 1995; nine senators fit the centrist category in 2004, compared with thirty-nine in 1995.[15] Such ideological solidarity, finally, is reinforced by the fact that congressmen run from districts that are increasingly homogeneous internally and heterogeneous externally: any district with large numbers of minority voters is as likely to be Democratic as any district with large numbers of exurban churchgoers is likely to be Republican.[16] Whether there is a cultural war in America with deep roots among ordinary people is debatable. Whether the United States is divided along partisan lines is not. In the new politics of democracy, political parties are less likely to resemble umbrella organizations and more likely to be extensions of the political movements that grew out of the 1960s.

Along with ideological certainty comes partisan regularity. Fifty years after the publication of a famous American Political Science Association report urging American political parties "to bring forth programs to which they commit themselves and . . . possess sufficient internal cohesion to carry out these programs," those parties are beginning to resemble Great Britain's, characterized by internal discipline and a determination to support (or oppose) the leader of both the party and the nation.[17] The Republican Party under George W. Bush fits this pattern most closely; it has developed a surprising ability to stay together on votes and to resist engaging in bipartisan negotiation with its opponents. As we saw in the previous chapter, Republicans can use their unity in Congress to govern without the annoying interference of a loyal opposition. Party government in America, which has always existed, has become partisan government in America, which is relatively new.

Being in the minority, Democrats have had little power to stop the Republicans from becoming more partisan. But they could, and did, become more partisan themselves. In 2005 Democrats in the House began to act in a far more unified fashion; they voted together 88 percent of the time, still below the Republicans by a couple of percentage points, but their highest degree of party unity ever.[18] Such partisan coherence paid immediate political dividends; not only were Democrats able to stop efforts at Social Security privatization, they joined with Republican defectors to pass a bill permitting federal funding of stem cell research; found themselves able to protect minimum wage laws against Republican efforts to suspend them in the wake of Hurricane Katrina; caused embarrassing delays in Republican efforts to secure a budget; and forced the president to expend significant political capital within his own party to obtain passage of the Central American Free Trade Agreement. A British-style system of party loyalty had crossed the legislative aisle. Such partisan unity may not last; indeed, to the degree that the Democrats are more unified in opposing President Bush, congressional Republicans, no longer able to run on his coattails, are less unified in supporting him. Still, to the surprise of those predicting the decline of political parties, partisanship has been flourishing in the first few years of the twenty-first century.

Partisanship serves a few important democratic functions: it allows for the expression of deeply held opinion, and, at least for those who identify with the dominant party, it enables those opinions to be translated into public policy. These are not insignificant virtues, but they do override other functions of the parties that used to be, and sometimes still are, cited in their defense. One of them—the capacity of parties to offer a sense of stability in an otherwise uncertain world—has been well expressed by Larry J. Sabato and Bruce A. Larson:

As mechanisms for organizing and containing political change, the parties are a potent force for stability. They represent continuity in the wake of
changing issues and personalities, anchoring the
electorate as the storms that are churned by new
political people and politics swirl around. Because
of its unyielding, pragmatic desire to win elections
(not just contest them), each party in a sense acts to
moderate public opinion. The party tames its own
extreme elements by pulling them toward an ideological center in order to attract a majority of votes
on election day.[19]

As a description of what political parties were able to do
during the old politics of democracy, this is apt. As an account
of the way parties operate in more ideological times, alas, it is
out of date. Because partisan parties activate the base more
than they mobilize the uncommitted, they energize extremists
far more than they tame them. Continuity is the last thing they
want if their objective is to change public policy in radically
new directions. Their goal, to be sure, is to win elections, but if
they can take steps to ensure their reelection by tampering
with district lines rather than actually contesting an opponent,
they will do that. They are not friends of stability if the price of
stability is bipartisan cooperation. Those in the majority certainly like holding political power and will do everything they
can to keep it. But for them the whole point of having political
power is not to realize an abstraction such as stability but to
achieve as much of their agenda as they can, even if one of the
consequences might well be greater instability in future years,
when they may no longer be in power.

Since stability is *not* the major objective of contemporary political parties, they also fail to carry out another function once held to have tremendous importance by students of political institutions: to act as a buffer between ordinary Americans and the government that speaks in their name.[20] When parties were organizationally stronger and more preoccupied with jobs and contracts than with causes and crusades, they offered numerous benefits to ordinary citizens, not just by providing tangible financial rewards but by cultivating a sense of political identity. As parties have become top-down institutions with a strong partisan focus, they serve needs having more to do with state and national office holders and their political agendas than with the concerns of voters. Seeing fewer benefits coming their way, ordinary citizens are likely to conclude that parties do not belong to them but are part of the Washington establishment for which they have so little veneration; 59 percent of Americans think that political parties have too much power, and a mind-boggling one-quarter of the American people would not mind seeing them banned.[21]

The more convinced Americans are that parties do not represent them, the more likely they are to adopt toward parties the same reasoning they apply to politics in general: the public distrusts the parties and turns against them, party leaders rely on precisely this public apathy or cynicism to further partisan goals, and this in turn proves to many Americans that they were right to view parties suspiciously in the first place. Parties that organize and represent public opinion have an important role to play in furthering a sense among ordinary citizens that politics is a legitimate activity. Those who preoccupy themselves with fashioning partisan and ideological agendas, by contrast, are less likely to be viewed by the public as a necessary component of democratic life and more likely to be characterized as out only for their own self-interest.

No one doubts that today's parties, and in particular the Republican Party, are superb machines for winning and holding political power. Whether they do so by strengthening the institutional infrastructure of American democracy is a more problematic proposition. Partisanship means putting parties first, which certainly sounds like a reasonable enough idea. But political parties in America have not always put partisanship first; sometimes they put country ahead of party and at other times they gave higher priority to the history and traditions of the branches of government to which they were elected than to the local and national party organizations that helped get them there. Conceived of as institutions designed to fight political wars, parties are flourishing. Imagined as institutions that help stabilize and secure American democracy, political parties are failing.

Interest groups are even more unpopular among Americans than political parties; in recent years, as a glance at Figure 1 suggests, as many as 75 percent of Americans have concluded that government is run by a few big interests, compared with as few as 20 percent who believe that its actions benefit all. In no other arena of American public life are the populist inclinations of Americans more pronounced than with regard to what people generally call the "special interests." One can point out in response that interest groups rely on freedom of speech and association guaranteed by the U.S. Constitution; that they frequently speak on behalf of large numbers of members, customers, or clients; that for every interest group lobbying in favor of a law's passage there are generally others mobilizing against it; or that interest groups can overplay their hand and lose. But none of these arguments seems to influence American opinion on the subject. Lobbying is as ubiquitous in American

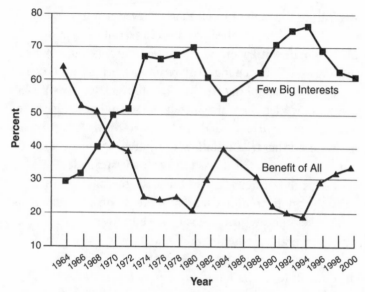

Figure 1. Survey responses to a question on whether government is
run by a few big interests or for the benefit of all, 1964–2000.
Source: National Election Studies, University of Michigan,
as compiled by David Lowery and Holly Brasher,
Organized Interests and American Government
(New York: McGraw Hill, 2004), 15.

democracy as it is unpopular. For those who uphold the importance of institutions in democratic performance, this is bad
news indeed. Americans ought to recognize that even if they
sometimes abuse their power, interest groups, like parties, play
an essential role in furthering such democratic goals as access,
representation, and accountability.

There was a time in the not too distant past when Americans gave proper appreciation to the role of interest groups; in
1964 twice as many Americans believed that the government

was run to the benefit of all than believed it was a captive of special interests. (The near complete reversal of opinion over the past half-century on the role interest groups play is one of the most striking changes in recent American politics.) It seems obvious, looking backward, that events such as Watergate and the Vietnam war, which increased public cynicism toward government, extended public distrust toward any organized interest that tries to influence what government does. Yet one wonders how fair it was to have made such a leap. It was, after all, private interests—in this case, the media—that enabled the public to understand how the Nixon administration had broken the law, just as it was cause-motivated groups that raised the issue of whether the Vietnam war was worth fighting. Private interests did more to protect democracy during the difficult 1970s than they did to undermine it.

Starting in about 1990, as Figure 1 also demonstrates, the proportion of Americans who believe that government is in the pocket of big interests began to decline, from roughly 75 percent to 60 percent, while the proportion of those who believe that government works to benefit all increased from 20 percent to 30 percent. This suggests some possible good news with respect to the role institutions play in a democracy: Americans may be starting to overcome their suspicions toward interest groups. The interesting question is whether interest groups are returning the favor by acting in ways that would justify this increasing confidence in what they do.

From the standpoint of legitimacy, the best contribution private interests groups make to democracy is to allow for access and representation but at the same time not to permit any one interest excessive access compared with others; without a widespread sense that fairness exists in political life, Americans are likely to conclude that their own interests are unrepresented, breeding cynicism and distrust. Political scientists use the term "pluralism" to describe a situation in which a variety of interests achieve effective access to government. There has long existed a debate over how pluralistic American democracy has been, and critics from E. E. Schattschneider to Charles Lindblom have concluded that even in a so-called pluralistic universe, business has a tendency to dominate government.[22] Yet neither Schattschneider nor Lindblom could have anticipated what came to be called the "K Street Project."

Named after the street on which many lobbyists have established their headquarters, the K Street Project was designed not only to allow lobbyists to make contributions to legislators in return for laws that benefit themselves—this has always been part of the politics of democracy—but to transform lobbying, which has usually been understood as bipartisan in nature, into an arm of one political party; in return for access to government, Republicans insisted that lobbying groups fire Democrats from their leadership positions and replace them with Republicans. The K Street Project found itself in deep political trouble when one of its key players, Jack Abramoff, turned state's evidence and began to reveal the names of congressmen who, he alleged, had taken money in return for favors. When Tom DeLay, one of the congressmen close to Abramoff, was forced to resign as majority leader, Republicans who sought his seat claimed that the days of the K Street Project would have to be brought to an end. Still, although Democrats will surely insist that lobbyists stop hiring only members of the majority party, no one seriously expects that lobbying will return to its once bipartisan days. The Republican Party finances itself by raising money from entrenched corporations in return for favorable policies, and that close link that has been established between lobbying and the needs of a particular party will easily survive all the talk of reform. Indeed, within months of the February 2006 election of Ohio's John Boehner to replace Tom DeLay as House majority leader, talk of reform had already died down.

Aligning interest groups along partisan lines may be an effective political tactic, but it undermines pluralism for two reasons. It is true, as Republicans are likely to insist, that their party did not invent the tendency to rely on powerful corporate interests for campaign cash; part of Bill Clinton's success was not only that he moved to the center on issues like welfare reform but that he, and his allies in groups such as the Democratic Leadership Council, made it clear that their party was not instinctively antibusiness. It harms pluralism to have two political parties substantially in debt to business, since business will have disproportionate influence whichever party is in power. But it harms pluralism even more if only one party has a special relationship with business, for if Democrats are excluded from lobbying, so are the non-business-oriented interests that cling to their party in greater numbers than they do to the Republicans.

In addition, Republicans who insist on a special relationship with lobbyists are not only bringing powerful interests into their party, they are also bringing them directly into a policy-making process, since, in the new politics of democracy, policy and politics have become so firmly interlinked. Under the terms of the K Street Project, business interests literally wrote drafts of the legislation expected to regulate them, a procedure also quite likely to survive, in one form or another, talk of reform. The danger of such a system is not only its obvious economic corruption but its political corruption as well. As is true of parties in more partisan times, interest groups in the new politics of democracy lose their capacity to act as a moderating force between ordinary citizens and the government that speaks in their name.

In important ways, the institutional dynamics of parties and interest groups have diverged. Parties, like so many other aspects of American political life, experienced a period of rapid democratization in the aftermath of the 1960s, while no such movement in favor of power from below ever touched America's major interest groups. As a consequence, parties lost some of their organizational tightness in recent years, while interest groups have become ever more centralized.

Yet what both have in common in the new politics of democracy is that they are increasingly transformed into Washington-based organizations with fewer, and more tenuous, ties to state and local affiliates. One sees this quite clearly when the issues at stake are religious and cultural. In the spirit of the new politics of democracy, conservatives like to claim that they are concerned with morality because they are responding to heartfelt demands from ordinary people for a return to traditional values. Yet not only is there not nearly as much popular support behind the culture war as the warriors themselves claim, many cultural and religious issues are fueled by what are increasingly called "Astroturf" organizations, named for the pioneer artificial-grass product. Astroturf organizations are Washington-based campaigns that simulate grassroots support but are in fact coordinated by ideological interest groups seeking particular legislative outcomes. In a fashion nearly identical to what is occurring in the realm of political parties, interest groups in the new politics of democracy activate more than they mobilize. This is most evident in the case of opposition to stem cell research, a cause that has little popular support. But even an issue such as gay marriage, which many Americans oppose, does not rank high on grassroots priority lists—certainly not to the extent of a demand for a constitutional amendment banning it, which activist interest groups within Washington's beltway favor. The trend in America, despite all the populistic rhetoric from politicians, is for issues to percolate from the top to the bottom, and this is as true with respect to ideologically motivated interest groups as it is with political parties.

To some degree, corporate interests should serve as a check on such top-down activation strategies. Their concerns, after all, are primarily financial in nature; they seek to increase the profits of the clients they serve and have little stake in the ideological battles over moral and cultural issues. Yet corporate resistance to the cultural war has been surprisingly muted. In part this is because President Bush has been able to name to the U.S. Supreme Court judges such as John Roberts and Samuel Alito, who appeal simultaneously to the religious right and to big business. In addition, corporate executives who feel no strong inclination to get involved in such issues as whether feeding tubes should be removed from brain-dead individuals or prayers should be said before high school football games are more likely to keep silent than to actively resist the agenda of the religious right. Corporations, which receive so many benefits from scientific innovation and tend to be guided more by pragmatism than by ideology in their search for new products, ought to serve as a source of resistance to crusades bent on teaching intelligent design or limiting the use of stem cells. That they so frequently fail to stand in the way of the culture warriors serves to show the remarkable degree to which the modern Republican Party has knit together a coalition of disparate interests. Whether this condition will prevail if deficits continue to expand or if even more drastic limits on scientific innovation are imposed is anyone's guess. To this point, however, remaining inside the Republican tent is more important to major corporate donors than advancing an agenda that gives a higher priority to innovation and growth than it does to religious conviction and moral certainty.

Interest groups continue to serve such democratic objectives as representation and freedom of association; for all their political power, they remain essentially private organizations exercising their rights to petition government on behalf of those they represent. What they do not offer in the new politics of democracy is anything resembling a goal of equal access. For those who believe that corporate interests in particular have so much power in the private sector that all others must turn to the public sector for protection against them, the domination of the public sector by corporate interests creates an additional level of access to the ones stemming from their economic resources. It may be reassuring for those who benefit from such a system to know that public skepticism toward interest groups is declining, for they can then claim public support for a system that disproportionately benefits private interests. But even at a time when antipathy toward interest groups is declining, there are still, as Figure 1 shows, twice as many Americans who believe in the essential unfairness of government as those who believe that it acts fairly—and this was before the name of Jack Abramoff was in the news. There are no easy methods of restoring public confidence in a political process that allows private interest groups to play important public functions, but it can hardly happen by stacking the deck in the interests of the most powerful and well financed, as is currently the case in Washington.

Americans do not view all forms of politics with suspicion. There is, in fact, one institution for which they express consid-

erable admiration; a whopping 84 percent of Americans think
it should be relied upon more often and only 16 percent do
not.[23] This great exception to American cynicism is the ballot
initiative. Americans love the idea that they themselves, without annoying and obstructionist intermediaries, should decide important matters of public policy. Direct democracy is as
widely admired in America as party and interest group democracy are distrusted.

Reforms such as ballot initiatives, referenda, and recalls
of public officials represent American anti-institutionalism in
something like its pure form. They are premised on the proposition that when it comes to matters involving tax reform, the
right to die, bilingual education, or even, in recall campaigns,
whether a politician recently elected should be unelected, the
voices of commonsense Americans ought to be given more
weight than the opinions of the experts and policy wonks. The
matters to be decided may sometimes be complex, but the answer is always simple: yes, or more frequently, no. In their discussion of the functions of political parties, Sabato and Larson
ask their readers to imagine what political life would look like
in their absence.[24] To some degree, we already know the answer. Elections would be dominated by ballot initiatives.

As befits the new politics of democracy, ballot initiatives,
which had been popular during the Progressive period, went
into a period of relative decline but then, as a result of the democratizing pressures of the 1960s, returned to and in many
cases exceeded earlier levels of popularity. The popularity of
ballot initiatives crosses all existing partisan and ideological
lines; California, Oregon, and Washington are all relatively liberal states, while Arizona and North Dakota are known as conservative ones, yet in both sets of states, direct democracy is
popular. Ballot initiatives are not, I hasten to add, ubiquitous in

all regions of the country; states that have historically not permitted them, from Rhode Island to Texas, are in no rush to do so. Still the fact that direct democracy initiatives are popular in states where political parties have historically been weak—California, Oregon, and Colorado hold roughly 40 percent of all the ballot initiatives in the U. S.[25]—suggests that an environment in which traditional political institutions are distrusted provides sustenance for the growth of nontraditional political institutions.

The question of whether initiatives and referenda improve democracy or worsen its performance is widely debated among political observers. Many are skeptical. "The initiative process," writes journalist David Broder, " . . . threatens to challenge or even subvert the American system of government in the next few decades," while for political scientist Richard J. Ellis, the popularity of these mechanisms represent "democratic delusions," especially the delusion that the hard work of politics and government can be avoided by simple appeals to the people.[26] Because they rely so explicitly on majority rule, others have pointed out, initiatives may unduly restrict the rights of racial minorities or immigrants.[27] And if excluded and stigmatized minorities are harmed by initiatives, powerful and well-financed minorities are helped by them, for they can, under appropriate circumstances, bypass legislatures entirely and take their self-interested causes directly to the electorate.[28]

Others find such concerns unwarranted. It is not necessarily true, they argue, that voters, faced with the technical and complicated language frequently found on such initiatives, have little idea what they are voting for; they are capable of responding to advertising and endorsements from political leaders that give them clues about the proper decisions for them to reach.[29] Nor should we conclude that powerful groups can get what

Table 4. Ballot Initiatives by Decade, Selected States

	1900s	1910s	1920s	1930s	1940s	1950s	1960s	1970s	1980s	1990s	2000–2004	Total
Alaska							2	7	8	13	8	38
Arizona		33	19	15	16	16	8	5	11	22	11	156
Arkansas		9	8	26	22	14	10	5	11	5	5	115
California	0	30	33	35	20	12	9	21	44	61	30	295
Colorado	0	37	18	19	9	8	9	19	15	37	18	189
Florida	0	0	0	0	0	0	0	2	4	9	12	27
Idaho	0	0	0	1	6	2	0	3	5	8	1	26
Illinois	0	0	0	0	0	0	0	0	1	0	0	1
Maine	0	1	2	3	2	0	0	4	12	11	9	44
Massachusetts	0	0	3	6	7	3	2	6	9	18	8	62
Michigan	0	3	3	16	5	4	1	11	8	6	6	63
Mississippi	0	0	0	0	0	0	0	0	0	2	0	2
Missouri	0	8	11	13	6	1	0	7	8	11	6	71

Montana	0	9	8	1	2	2	1	9	16	16	7	71
Nebraska	0	4	1	7	5	3	4	2	3	10	6	45
Nevada	0	1	1	3	1	6	2	1	8	13	10	46
North Dakota	0	7	25	45	21	17	14	11	11	19	3	173
Ohio	0	13	7	6	3	2	2	12	7	8	2	62
Oklahoma	1	17	8	16	9	6	10	5	4	8	1	85
Oregon	23	82	28	26	14	14	7	18	32	56	31	331
South Dakota	1	7	6	0	1	1	0	6	13	10	6	51
Utah	0	0	0	0	0	2	1	3	6	3	4	19
Washington	0	9	5	16	9	13	13	20	14	29	16	144
Wyoming	0	0	0	0	0	0	0	0	0	7	0	7
Total	25	270	186	254	158	126	95	177	250	382	200	2,123

Source: Richard J. Ellis, *Democratic Delusions: The Initiative Process in America* (Lawrence: University Press of Kansas, 2002), 206 (data recalculated by author), supplemented by various Web pages of secretaries of state, state governments.

they want by raising the funds to put initiatives on the ballot; they still have to convince a majority of the voters to back their propositions.[30] Ballot initiatives, it has been found, increase political knowledge among voters and contribute to a sense of greater efficacy.[31] And although the evidence is not conclusive, ballot propositions may increase voter turnout and in that sense help overcome apathy.[32] All in all, one scholar concludes, the statistical evidence is overwhelming: "the initiative pushes policy in the direction a majority of the people say they want to go."[33]

Still, the arguments and data on both sides leave the issue undecided. And this is because the interesting question with respect to ballot initiatives is not whether they work well but whether they live up to the expectations that Americans have of them. Americans clearly like direct democracy because they believe it will give the people more of a say in politics than they obtain when intermediaries such as parties and interest groups act on their behalf. But even if initiatives work better than their critics believe, they still are bound to dissatisfy a public with unrealistic expectations about what politics can do. Direct democracy almost never produces the better political world it promises.

Consider just the sheer amount of cash it takes to get an initiative on the ballot and win public support for it. The need for money benefits those who have the resources, which means that even if well-financed interests do not win all the time, they still establish the agenda: casino interests have been single minded in their determination to expand their industry through ballot initiatives in California and Missouri, organized labor is especially active in Oregon, and an emerging stem cell industry wrote the initiative allowing California to support scientific research in that hot field. Enthusiasts for ballot initiatives view them as an alternative to politics as usual, but politicians themselves frequently call for and support ballot initiatives when they fear their programs may not win legislative support. Signature gathering has become an industry in itself; initiatives do not get on the ballot because dedicated volunteers ask shoppers to sign a petition in front of their local supermarket but because supporters turn immediately to firms that specialize in obtaining signatures. Ballot initiatives, because of their cost, rely on the media to an usual degree, and so long as media advertising contains its share of negative accusations and one-sided story telling, which in initiative campaigns it frequently does, initiatives can contribute to public disgust with politics in general.

And then there is the coup de grace: for all their popularity with Americans, initiatives do not always initiate. Between 1960 and 1999, 65 percent of the initiatives passed in California were challenged in the courts, and only a minority of those challenges were dismissed.[34] Other initiatives are routinely ignored by legislators after they are passed, especially if the expenditure of funds is required. And some initiatives could never be implemented even if the legislative or administrative desire was there to do so: immigration will not stop after voters proclaim that it should, taxes continue to be raised after tax limitations initiatives pass, and tough measures against crime rarely influence the crime rate. It would be difficult to find a political process more likely to reinforce public cynicism than one which raises the hopes of a not well informed public that life will improve if they take matters into their own hands only to discover, once they do, that nothing much changes.

Even if they are responsive to the public policy preferences of Americans, in short, initiatives both contribute to and reinforce the problems of the new politics of democracy. States that rely upon them experience more than their share of symbolic politics: highly charged and emotionally laden issues that call upon the public to express indignation without offering much in the way of actual policies more likely to be responsive to their actual needs. Conflict-drenched intransigence at the ballot box becomes a substitute for compromise-induced moderation in the legislature. Legislation can be passed without legislators, but when that happens, the crucial role of writing laws passes to others, including those with a direct stake in the outcome, making it that much more difficult to hold decision-makers accountable for their actions. The recall enables voters to force office holders into retirement, but no sooner are they used than the public begins to tire of their replacements. Far from giving Americans a say over what happens in their name, direct democracy is one more indication of the way Americans avoid politics by transforming it into melodrama.

This does not mean that direct democracy is without friends. On the contrary, an atmosphere in which politicians routinely rush to praise the good sense of the ordinary voter is one that breeds ever greater reliance on ballot initiatives. And no one is quicker to praise such initiatives more than the right-wing culture warriors who thrive under the requisites of the new politics of democracy. Political scientist Richard Ellis points out that the two great movements pushing direct democracy forward are libertarianism, which tells people that government is not needed, and populism, which informs them that it cannot be trusted. Link libertarianism with populism and you get a figure such as conservative activist Grover Norquist, along with Karl Rove as responsible for conservative success in the new politics of democracy as any person in America.

Norquist, not surprisingly, is a big fan of direct democracy. He has written that "one big difference between initiatives and elected representatives is that initiatives do not change their minds once you vote them in."[35] He may be right, but, then again, one of the features that makes democracy healthy is that people ought to change their minds as they learn new things about the world around them. Norquist's comment is a new perfect illustration of the extent to which conservative populists thrive on responsiveness in government: the people tell their leaders what to do and they do it. And they just as well indicate why initiatives and referenda, for all their seemingly democratic nature, undermine political accountability; once the people authorize a change, they need no longer pay much attention to whether anyone is carrying out their wish. Norquist's views about direct democracy offer, not a formula for good or wise government, but for public policy formed by emotions, the more raw and uninformed the emotions, the better.

Inspired by Tocqueville, the first to call attention to the enormously important role institutions play in a democracy, contemporary political scientists frequently bemoan the impoverished state of civic life in the United States. There is certainly cause for their gloom. Democracy, as I have been arguing throughout this book, is not working as well as it could—and should. Voters lack knowledge of the positions held by those for whom they vote. Lacking such knowledge, it becomes difficult for them to hold leaders accountable for the decisions they make. And the very institutions to which Tocqueville pointed as expressions of the spirit of voluntarism are losing their attachments to the grass roots. The new politics of democracy claims to speak in the name of the people, but the people do not seem happy with the result.

One frequently attributed cause for America's civic impoverishment is widespread radical individualism, the pervasive idea that Americans should rely primarily on themselves. It is because they like individualism so much that Americans dislike collectivism so thoroughly. Government ought always to be treated with a degree of skepticism, they believe, and since institutions such as political parties and interest groups are, in their view, so close to government, the same suspicion ought to be extended to them.

It may surprise Americans to learn that their distrust of political institutions actually strengthens the government they so widely dislike. Radical individualism and strong political authority do not stand in opposition to each other, one reason why the extremely conservative administrations of both Ronald Reagan and George W. Bush wound up expanding the government they hoped to shrink. Modern society simply cannot function as it does without assembling individuals into collectivities capable of engaging in large-scale projects—from building roads to fighting wars—that no individual alone can do. Institutions that exist between the individual and the state offer one form of collective action that avoids both anarchism on the one hand and oppressive government on the other. Weaken the capacity of such institutions to act, and some other collective institution—invariably the one called government—will step in.

When Americans bypass institutions in favor of either private apathy or such ultimately unsatisfying forms of public activity as the referendum and the recall, they certainly have more freedom to do what they want; they can throw duly elected politicians out of office or they can demand laws as impractical to administer as they are simplistic in intent. Paradoxically, however, the same freedom that allows Americans to do what they want also gives government more freedom to do what it wants, for long after the public attention has flagged,

someone in authority will have to implement what the public
desires or provide reasons why it cannot be done. It can hardly
be surprising that a political movement as populistic and lib-
ertarian in rhetoric as today's Republican Party in practice pre-
sides over an expansion of government even more dramatic
than those associated with Democrats. Only at a time in which
political knowledge is scant, democratic accountability weak,
and institutions hollowed out can you find a Grover Norquist
(the activist who wishes to flush government down the toilet)
existing in the same political party as a John Yoo (the presidential adviser who argued for the president's inherent authority to do anything he wanted in the war on terror, including allowing the government to poke into the most intimate of
people's private affairs). It was once a staple of political wisdom that when individual freedom expands, the state's authority constricts and vice versa. In reality, increased libertarianism and stronger and more intrusive government are both
by-products of a society in which intermediating institutions
find it difficult to carry out their tasks.

V

Democracy Without Disinterest

Democratic societies require political parties and interest groups because such institutions allow for the expression of interest; through them, individuals and groups that know what they want and are determined to realize what best serves their own needs can make their demands heard. As important as institutions that allow for the expression of self-interest may be for democratic performance, they also, if they are to avoid a Hobbesian war of all against all, need to be accompanied by institutions that embody a spirit of disinterest. Sports fans understand that highly competitive games taking place without referees would degenerate into chaos. Like sports, politics—equally competitive but with higher stakes—requires timekeepers, officials, traditions, and even whistle-blowers, all designed to assure that no one can bend the rules to his advantage. In a democracy, self-interested many institutions can be, but disinterested at least some must be.

American democracy would face serious problems of quality control if just one of its institutions of disinterest were to find itself unable to exercise neutral judgment. Yet in the new politics of democracy, nearly every one of the institutions America once counted on to stand above contending political and economic forces is finding it more difficult to do so. By their very nature, disinterested institutions have weak constituencies in a society governed by the principle of self-interest. That they lasted as long as they did in the United States is remarkable. But they are now increasingly hard to find, and there is no sign that they will be revived in the near future.

Beginning a discussion of the importance of disinterested institutions with the media may seem an odd choice. Most people take media bias as a fact of life; the right is convinced that the media are dominated by the left, while the left is certain that they are controlled by the right.[1] Yet under the rules of the old politics of democracy, newspapers, radio, and television considered themselves industries with no particular viewpoint other than dedication to the public welfare.

It is "inconceivable that we should allow so great a possibility for service, for news, for entertainment, for education and for vital commercial purposes to be drowned in advertising chatter."[2] Speaking is not a public television executive from Massachusetts but Herbert Hoover, later one of America's most conservative presidents, at a 1922 conference discussing the future of radio. As the sociologist Paul Starr has written, a general consensus against advertising on radio was so strong in the 1920s that the advertising industry supported it. Radio would be a private industry designed to make a profit, but it would not be subject to the self-interested principles of laissez-faire that generally governed all other forms of business activity.

These days even "noncommercial" public television, which announces its corporate underwriters before its news broadcasts, features more advertising than commercial radio did when it began. Yet although commercialization had become a fact of life for the American media by the 1930s, the notion that this industry should be different from all other industries persisted well into contemporary times. "To the extent that radio and television are mass media of entertainment," wrote CBS News President Richard Salant in 1976, "it is entirely proper to give most of the people what most of them want most of the time. But we in broadcast journalism cannot, should not, and will not base our judgments on what we think viewers and listeners are 'most interested' in, or hinge our news judgment and our news treatment on our guesses as to what news the people want to hear or see."[3] To a certain degree, Salant's commitment to providing news based on professional judgment rather than popular taste was self-interested. Airwaves were precious commodities, and so long as media companies were dependent upon licenses that enabled them to use the airwaves, prestigious news broadcasting, even if unprofitable, was the price to be paid for public legitimacy. Still, viewers of commercial news broadcasts at the time Salant made his comment were exposed to stories that focused disproportionately on "hard news," events involving public affairs, economics, or international relations.

Three economic transformations rendered Salant's views obsolete within a decade of his pronouncement: corporate acquisitions that enabled nonmedia companies to own media outlets; deregulation on the part of the Federal Communications Commission that reduced the need for "prestige" broadcasting; and the rise of competition from cable networks. The inevitable result was the decision by all three major networks to feature ever more news items fashioned to public taste. To cite just one example, soft news segments, like those featuring a prominent celebrity, increased from 26.4 percent of CBS's news stories in the 1974–1978 period to 46.8 percent in the period from 1994 to 1998, while coverage of key congressional votes declined from 81.1 percent of those identified as important by *Congressional Quarterly* to 60 percent. (CBS is known for its greater commitment to hard news than the other networks, though under the recent leadership of Leslie Moonves, it has been shedding that commitment; by contrast, ABC reported on only 50 percent of the important congressional votes and NBC 52.9 percent.)[4] When economics assumes increasing importance in broadcasting decisions, networks will pay less attention to foreign affairs, as well as to important but unglamorous aspects of domestic politics, for the simple reason that such unpopular subjects are less likely to recover the costs of production.

The media's move away from hard news, precipitated by economic factors, worked remarkably hand in glove with the political changes taking place in the United States during the same time period. Populistic politics helped cause, and in turn was strengthened by, the breakup of once-monopolistic outlets in favor of a competitive environment that required media firms to spend more time finding out what audiences wanted and to give it to them. Culture war politics provided nearly perfect grist for an industry seeking to find ways to make political debate more audience friendly to a citizenry not intent on grasping the complexities of public policy. Take economic factors such as media deregulation and add to them the new politics of democracy, and the outcome is *The O'Reilly Factor*.

A more competitive media environment may be more audience friendly, but it is highly unlikely to improve the quality of democratic life. The kinds of programming featured in this media environment certainly do not. James T. Hamilton,

the economist who has most carefully studied these developments, points out that "programs associated with hard news
content attract audiences that are politically active and knowledgeable, while those associated with soft news attract viewers
who are less interested in and active in politics."[5] Greater reliance on human interest stories and tales of government waste
on national television, it would seem, like weather forecasts
and reports of accidents on local news, contribute to the already substantial level of political ignorance in the United
States, as well as to increased cynicism and declining participation. In search of expanded market share, television needs the
marginal viewer for the same reason that politicians seek the
marginal voter, resulting in the same perverse consequence:
the less you know and care about politics, the more interested
the media are in appealing to your emotions.

It was not just programming that was influenced by this
conjuncture of economic and political transformations; traditional assumptions about the relationship between the media
and the public were challenged as well. It is a staple of politics
that any political party or ideological movement, to the degree
that it can, will try to shape the news in its favor. At the same
time, however, liberals and conservatives tend to think of the
role of disinterested news in different ways. Liberal thinkers
from Immanuel Kant to John Rawls and Jürgen Habermas
have long insisted on the importance of a position of disinterest from which all political points of view, including liberalism
itself, can be judged. Conservatives, by contrast, especially
those writing in the shadow of Machiavelli and German theorists of realpolitik, have argued that politics is much like warfare and that such a thing as neutrality is impossible. (In recent
times leftists attracted to postmodernism have joined conservatives on this point.)

These different attitudes toward the possibility of neutrality spill over into contemporary political debates about the media. When liberals look at efforts to provide the public more information, set events into context, or editorialize on behalf of the common good, they see attempts to speak in disinterested fashion on behalf of the nation's conscience. Conservatives look at those very same efforts and see liberalism run amok; providing information is in their view little more than dismissing the rock-ribbed beliefs of ordinary Americans; contextualizing events amounts to what conservatives, including George W. Bush, frequently denounce as "filtering"; and what liberals insist is good for the country is to conservatives little more than what is good for liberals. The liberal ideal is a widely admired figure like Walter Cronkite telling Americans unpleasant but necessary truths. The conservative ideal is a cable news program that makes no pretense of objectivity but presents a free-for-all across the ideological spectrum in order to allow people to make up their own minds.

As American news media became more competitive, more preoccupied with the bottom line, and more determined to hold on to their audience share, they also became more vulnerable to conservative attacks on their presumed neutrality. For all their talk about liberal bias in the media, conservatives have come to dominate the flow of political information; they have their own television network, Fox News; they offer their own major newspaper editorial page in the *Wall Street Journal;* they literally monopolize talk radio in every region of the country; and they have even been successful at introducing conservative voices into public radio and television, long their bêtes noires. The true extent of the conservative victory, however, lies not in the greater visibility of right-wing points of view in the new politics of democracy but in the way in which all media, and not just conservative media, treat opinion. It is the conservative model—ideological argumentation based on talking points, appeals to the like-minded rather than efforts to persuade, name-calling, sometimes to the point of character assassination—that has won the war for how news should be presented, not the liberal ideal of disinterested authority searching for a point above the fray.

The conservative view of how news should be presented has much to recommend it. Conservatives have detected all too many examples of liberal partisanship masquerading as objective journalism, none more notorious than the doctored stories run on CBS concerning President George W. Bush's national guard duty. Vigorous debate between committed partisans, moreover, contributes to the responsiveness (if not, alas, the accountability) that characterizes the new politics of democracy: such debate makes clear to all that more than one point of view exists, places a premium upon instant response, and shifts the ultimate authority for determining winners and losers away from broadcasters to the viewing public itself. And whatever one thinks of the era in which the average television set had seven channels and one-third of all Americans watched the evening news, media technology is too dynamic to stand still; given the opportunity to get their news in all kinds of new ways, most Americans will take advantage of it.

At the same time, however, more partisan news coverage and commentary also reinforce the same trends toward declining quality visible in other aspects of the new politics of democracy. You do not need to be informed to have an opinion as you watch partisan television; passion counts more than fact when the give-and-take is fast and furious. Even on the most partisan networks, you will be exposed to a point of view other than your own, but the constant reiteration of talking points, infrequent changes of mind, and endless spin and counterspin contribute to forms of hard-edged cynicism which conclude that everyone is out for himself. The idea that the people should decide who wins and loses these media slugfests works in roughly the same fashion as the notion that market share should determine what gets featured in the first place. Ultimately, it is the very populism of the new media, and in particular its market-driven efforts to give people what they most want, that undermines the ability of news providers to take a longer view, to represent what might be in the public interest, to educate their audience as well as entertain it, and to act as the conscience of the society.

When it first appeared on the scene, the Internet held out a promise of democratic revitalization. As it has evolved, however, Internet communication has developed into a nearly perfect technology for the ideological, take-no-quarters style of debate that characterizes the new politics of democracy. As the legal theorist Cass Sunstein argues, one of the Internet's major attractions—he calls it "The Daily Me"—is that it permits any person to customize his or her preferences, choosing news only from trusted sources and avoiding information that might be foreign or unpleasant.[6] The whole notion has an intuitive appeal, but only, Sunstein continues, if we view freedom as the absence of restraint. Freedom also involves being able to take advantage of opportunities, and if such opportunities are closed to us, we are less free as a result. That is why Sunstein thinks it is wrong to assume that the preferences people express are necessarily the only ones they have; you cannot know what you might prefer if you never have had the chance to prefer it. By tailoring news to our personal tastes, the Internet is highly democratic in one sense: there are blogs that cater to all shades of opinion on both the left and the right, and you, the reader, get to pick the ones that most appeal to you. But in another sense, the Internet is not democratic at all: it makes it as hard to be exposed to unfamiliar points of view as it makes it easy to reinforce the views we already have. Government, in Sunstein's view, would best serve the cause of democracy not by abandoning its role in the regulation of media but by trying to ensure that people have access to as much information as possible while remaining neutral between the points of view associated with them.

The media may once have been considered an industry with special responsibilities toward the public welfare, but the combined effect of these changes in politics and economics have turned this industry into one that copies, rather than covers, the culture war. Media in America have taken the true proposition that disinterested objectivity is difficult and translated it into the false proposition that disinterested objectivity is impossible. Television and radio are certainly more entertaining than they were when the media aimed to be above the fray, and Internet blogging has added a degree of responsiveness to politics that was not there when communication time moved so much slower. But without an appeal to disinterest the media are also more coarse, demeaning, superficial, and extremist. Technologically speaking, the American media offer the prospect of more democracy. Qualitatively speaking, they leave Americans frustrated and angry rather than engaged and efficacious, thereby contributing to the very skepticism about disinterested institutions that might otherwise contribute to improved democratic performance.

On the afternoon of March 25, 1968, a group of foreign policy officials, including many of those who had fashioned America's entry into the cold war twenty years earlier, met at the State Department. Their mission was to be briefed on the state of U.S. involvement in Vietnam and to recommend to President Johnson a possible course for the United States to follow. The next morning the elder statesman of the group that has come to be called the Wise Men, former Secretary of State Dean Acheson, told the president, "We can no longer do the job we set out to do in the time we have left, and we must take steps to disengage."[7] Johnson was not happy with the advice he received, and he did not disengage. But the seeds were planted that eventually resulted in the withdrawal of American troops.

Nearly forty years later, on January 5, 2006, a similar meeting took place in Washington. Invited to the White House by President Bush were thirteen former secretaries of state and defense, all there to discuss foreign policy with the president.[8] This time, however, no seeds seem to have been planted that would lead to a reexamination of presidential policies, especially those concerning the war in Iraq. The president allowed the group only five or ten minutes of discussion before leading them to a photo op. The only words that seemed to spark an exchange were uttered by former Secretary of State Madeleine Albright, who asked whether the president's preoccupation with Iraq was not leading him to pay insufficient attention to other threats to American interests. "I can't let this comment stand," President Bush responded, before telling the group that his administration was quite capable of doing more than one thing at a time. The whole event seemed designed to counter the criticism that President Bush lived in a bubble. The collected wisdom in the room was not being tapped for any serious advice about how to overcome the problems posed for American foreign policy by the Iraqi war.

Except for those who believe that the United States ought to have persevered in Vietnam until it won, history, as their sobriquet suggests, has judged the Wise Men of 1968 kindly. Wise though they may have been, these men were nonetheless very much at odds with the democratizing spirit of their times. They were, for one thing, all men, and white, Christian ones at that. Even though they served their country well, they represented no one but themselves. Living exemplars of what was frequently called the Establishment, they either ignored or, in the case of George F. Kennan, were disgusted by, the tastes and lifestyles of ordinary Americans. Nearly all of them had made their careers in appointed, rather than elected, positions. Public opinion was already turning against the war in Vietnam at the time the Wise Men made their pronouncements, no doubt an advantage to them as they pressed their case. Still, it was considered a serious violation of the rules that governed politics at the time they met to challenge the views of an elected president, and to take that step, they had to manifest a significant degree of political courage.

President Bush, by contrast, no doubt believed that he was justified in treating his meeting with former foreign policy officials as simply a public relations gesture. Americans, he liked to point out in good populistic fashion after his reelection in 2004, had been presented with two different courses of action with respect to foreign policy during the campaign and, by choosing him, they had endorsed one of them. From Mr. Bush's point of view, the people had spoken and the case was closed. But by aligning himself with the gut instincts of public opinion and ignoring the advice of bipartisan experts, Mr. Bush reinforced the views of those who believed his administration to be inflexible, uninterested in views that ran counter to its deeply ingrained convictions about the world, and unwilling to tolerate dissent from within or without. Now that the war in Iraq increasingly resembles the one in Vietnam in both its futility and its possibility of defeat, the popular course endorsed by the voters will probably turn out to have been precisely the wrong way to strengthen U.S. national security. No wonder, then, that such establishment types as Brent Scowcroft, Lawrence Wilkerson, the former chief of staff for Secretary of State Colin Powell, and numerous retired generals have broken with the gentlemanly code of the foreign policy establishment with their frequently pungent criticism of President Bush and Vice President Cheney.

Two wars, and two different reactions to them, illustrate what John Judis has called the paradox of American democracy.[9] As odd as it may sound to contemporary ears, democracy works best when elites are visible and influential, and it works poorly when they are not. Elites, to be sure, are privileged in lifestyle and unusually well connected. But in taking a long-term view of what society needs, they typically stand above the fray of clashing interests and parties. From this position of relative disinterest, they can provide democracy with two qualities it would otherwise lack: pluralism and pragmatism.

Pluralism is important to democracy because it represents the most effective way to deliver fairness. In a market-driven society such as the United States, business will nearly always be in a position to receive a disproportionate share of the benefits of public policy. In general, Americans do not object to probusiness policies, but there nonetheless have been times in the course of American history when the share going to business became so much greater than the share going to anyone else—the Gilded Age of the late nineteenth century, the years immediately preceding the Great Depression—that Americans began to lose faith in the fundamental fairness of their society, sometimes to the point of joining radical movements of opposition. The response of elites who founded organizations such as the National Civic Federation, the Ford and Rockefeller Foundations, or the Brookings Institution was to invite labor leaders, church figures, and academic experts to participate, along with business, in a search for policies that represented the general interest and not the specific needs of a particular industry or firm. Pluralistic democracy—a political system in which many different groups were allowed to compete with business for governmental benefits—could not occur naturally, or so they believed. It required leadership to bring pluralism into being, and that leadership would be provided by the elite.

By their very nature, pluralistic public policies are also pragmatic. Although businessmen are exceptionally practical people in their commercial activities, they frequently defer to ideology in their public posture; the laws of laissez-faire, they will insist, doom to failure any effort to bring government onto the side of labor or consumers (even as business brings government onto its side whenever it can). By forcing public policy to confront actual facts—how many Americans live in poverty? how extensive is racial discrimination in the workplace? what constitutes a healthy diet?—elite organizations try to shift democracy's conversation away from ideological confrontation into an often overly technical (and frequently difficult to understand) focus on consequences. It was because elite organizations were so important to the politics of the 1950s and 1960s that John F. Kennedy, in a commencement speech at Yale University in 1962, could conclude that "the central domestic problems of our time . . . do not relate to basic clashes of philosophy and ideology, but to ways and means of recasting common goals—to research for sophisticated solutions to complex and obstinate issues."[10]

These same qualities of pluralism and pragmatism also influenced the conduct of American foreign policy, especially when such elite organizations as the Council on Foreign Relations played an important role. Just as pluralism requires that voices other than the dominant one of business be heard, effective diplomacy demands that a powerful country such as the United States be willing to listen to, and even to try to take into account, the views of less powerful allies; elites open to international opinion and widely connected to similarly minded individuals in other countries could act as a check upon the tendency of the United States to go it alone in the world, whether by withdrawing into isolationism or by insisting on its unilateralist prerogatives. And a more pluralistic foreign policy, like its domestic counterpart, would also be more pragmatic; its language would be realistic rather than moralistic, seeking managerial solutions to confront America's enemies as an alternative to an ideological war against their way of life. In spite of this commitment to pragmatism, it must be said, the foreign policy elite that assumed so much prominence during the Kennedy administration managed to get the United States involved over its head in Vietnam. But then again, as the experience of the Wise Men suggests, it also took giant steps to help get the United States out.

Elites typically flourished among prominent New England families imbued with a sense of noblesse oblige. Besides foundations and think tanks, they assumed leadership positions at public television stations, museums, libraries, Ivy League universities, and civic organizations with names such as Common Cause. Elites frequently served as trustees for these organizations, and the term "trustee" captures their understanding of how politics should work. If they do their jobs well, trustees are responsible for the overall health of the institution on whose board they sit, not to the interests of the particular leadership of that institution at any given moment in time. Trustees believe themselves insulated from pressures coming from customers, alumni, donors, or suppliers. What trustees call "public service" comes naturally to them; the country needs them more than the country club, they will insist, and when a president asks them to accept the low salary and long hours that came along with a high government position, their sense of duty does not permit them to say no. At times an elite can become so disinterested that it is willing to attack itself; in perhaps the quintessential act of self-sacrifice on the part of the American elite, Kingman Brewster, longtime president of Yale University, decided that the country would be better off if its leadership were more diverse and open to experience, and led a campaign to strip Yale of much of the influence of people whose primary claim to leadership was inheritance.[11]

Brewster, as matters turned out, was right to anticipate an era in which the establishment would lose its clout. All the democratic trends of the 1960s and 1970s contributed to the declining influence of the elite. Geographically, Americans began moving west, where breeding counts less than innate ability. Politically, the policies of "the best and the brightest" failed not only in Vietnam but in the inner cities, fueling a backlash against the elite's sense of entitlement. Socially, the children of the elite, frequently paralyzed with guilt, were uninterested or unwilling to take their place in an establishment even if such a place were still available. Militarily, the United States began to turn away from Europe, where elite connections were strong, to Asia and the Middle East, where they were weak. Economically, business interests, in a more competitive corporate environment, lobbied increasingly for what was in their own interest rather than what might be in the national interest. Elites, in short, eventually had to answer the omnipresent call of populism, and when they did, they could no longer consider themselves elites.

Before conservatives had learned the attractions of populism, they might have been expected to rally to the defense of an anointed and socially prominent establishment. Instead, the dynamics of the new politics of democracy enabled conservatives to welcome the decline of the elite because it represented to them the collapse of liberalism. If liberal elites wanted to destroy any influence they had by moving closer to the counterculture and the New Left, that was fine from the viewpoint of the increasingly influential neoconservatives; they would simply ignore such once-elite institutions as Ivy League universities and the Council on Foreign Relations and create their own institutions. In their years out of office, especially during the presidencies of Jimmy Carter and Bill Clinton, conservative activists did exactly that, establishing an impressive number of think tanks, advocacy organizations, and lobbying groups designed to advance their goals. The differences in leadership style between these organizations and those of the northeastern establishment have been well described by John Judis:

> The new groups, in contrast to the old, did not seek to be above class, party, and ideology. On the contrary, they were openly probusiness and conservative. . . . They did not seek to mediate conflicts, but to take one side. They had no ties to labor unions or to the environmental, consumer or civil rights movements that had emerged in the sixties, but only to the business counteroffensive against them. . . . They did not seek to produce objective results by means of social science. On the contrary, they were willing to use social science to achieve partisan results.

It is tempting to conclude that with the emergence of the new politics of democracy, a tired and liberal elite had been replaced by an aggressive and conservative one. But if an elite is defined by its commitment to the principle of disinterest, then Judis is right to conclude of these kind of men that "instead of creating a new elite, they undermined what it meant for the country to have an elite."[12]

Now that disinterested elites have lost so much influence in the new politics of democracy, the two qualities they offered democracy—pluralism and pragmatism—are in short supply. Hostile to notions of pluralism, America's conservative policy makers seek to benefit the already well-off in domestic life just as, in international affairs, they insist that no other country should ever be allowed to challenge the already considerable power of the United States. Convinced that their version of the truth is the only credible one, moreover, they justify their policies based on an ideological view that seeks to change the world rather than to manage it. Their antielitism is not just a pose. Conservative leaders of the new politics of democracy sometimes imagine themselves as revolutionary, and rightly so. They look back on an era in which disinterested advice was prevalent and recoil in horror.

None of this is a problem if one believes that democracy is best served when those in power respond as promptly as possible to the views of those who put them there, even if those views are as uninformed as they are motivated by frustration or anger. But if one believes that democracy works best when the actions of its leaders are not only responsive but also wise, then problems abound. A wise society seeks to base its policies on the best available knowledge of how they might work. It includes as many people within the scope of its benefits as necessary to ensure that its policies will be perceived as legitimate.

It seeks to form consensus to avoid the bad faith and ugly vituperation associated with political extremism. By no longer heeding the voice of elites whose relative disinterest could bring such wisdom to the conduct of its affairs, American democracy suffers from a serious, if self-inflicted, wound.

As befits a society given to the notion that it is governed by laws rather than men, American courts in general, and the U.S. Supreme Court in particular, were, a generation or two ago, viewed as places in which partisan politics would play a secondary role; law professors concerned themselves with finding neutral principles for constitutional adjudication; scholars and justices took pride in their ability to separate what the law required from their own political convictions; and presidents sought to appoint highly qualified people to the bench, whether or not the political views of those appointees were in perfect accord with their own.[13] This commitment to dispassionate justice could not, and did not, prevent the Warren Court from reaching some very liberal, and highly controversial, decisions, just as it did not stop conservative critics from mobilizing their forces in opposition. Yet under the old politics of democracy there nonetheless existed a widespread consensus that politics and law were two different things. Judicial review ceded to the Supreme Court an enormous amount of power; it could declare unconstitutional the actions of the other branches of government. And like members of any other branch of government, justices followed public opinion, even if indirectly. Still, justices lacked the authority to enforce their decisions and could not, on their own, initiate legislation; for these reasons alone, even the most passionately political of them recognized that their legitimacy was dependent on their ability to remain above partisan rancor.

Partisan rancor today is more or less a synonym for the process of judicial nominations. For American conservatives, the failure of the U.S. Senate to confirm the appointment of Robert Bork to the Supreme Court in 1987 started all the fuss. Bork, they insist, was supremely qualified; Democratic opposition was based strictly on contempt for his political views; and by his rejection conservatives were thus given every reason to oppose the nomination of liberal judges by liberal presidents. As Ethan Bronner's history of the Bork controversy makes clear, liberals did indeed turn the Bork nomination into an ideological crusade.[14] Yet although liberals frequently acted badly during the episode, one wonders how long the Bork affair will be permitted to reverberate. Bork himself, in the years after his nomination, demonstrated far more of an ideological than a judicial temperament in his best-selling books, suggesting that he was not fit for the Court in the first place. And even though he was denied a seat, two equally conservative justices, Antonin Scalia and Clarence Thomas, not only were seated but later played a visible role in the Supreme Court decision that paved the way for the presidency of George W. Bush. Safely reelected, Mr. Bush, in turn, was able to name to the Court two judges, John Roberts and Samuel Alito, widely admired by conservatives of all stripes. If conservatives are entitled for some payback for the way liberals treated Robert Bork, they certainly have gotten it. Still, there will always be new justices to appoint, both to the Supreme Court and to lower federal courts, and every indication suggests that Republicans will consider ideology in selecting them, just as Democrats will rate ideology as a criterion for opposing them.

If you are a liberal, you obviously do not like the fact that the American judiciary has tilted so far to the right. Yet the real loss that flows from the politicization of the judiciary is one of ideas, including many conservative ideas, that would have enabled a Supreme Court decision to be accepted as legitimate by all sides. The most important of those ideas is judicial restraint, which, broadly speaking, means that justices should, as much as possible, defer to the will of the elected branches of government. Judicial restraint was once the fundamental disposition of such liberal justices as Felix Frankfurter and Alexander Bickel. Conservatives as well once paid frequent homage to restraint; allowing judicial opinions to be guided by the original intent of the writers of the Constitution, as Robert Bork said they should be, was meant to limit the ability of judges to legislate from the bench. If only Bork's theory had held, some of the fierce battles over the judiciary in the United States might have been avoided.

The theory, alas, did not hold. Conservatives did not fight furious battles to get more of their ideological kin on the Supreme Court just to see them restrained. They had specific political objectives in mind; in particular, they wanted to see free-market economic principles flourish and to return more power to the states (even if, on issues such as assisted suicide, they also wanted the federal government to have the last word). To achieve those objectives, judges would have to be willing to declare laws regulating business or centralizing authority in the federal government unconstitutional, even if doing so would be little different from the Warren Court's attempts to declare laws abridging privacy or criminal rights unconstitutional. This was not a temptation conservatives were prepared to resist; on the contrary, they showed less restraint than the Warren Court, which had in its most active years, struck down an average of 2.29 federal statues a year, compared with the 3.6 of the Rehnquist Court of 1995–2005.[15] The reason why is not hard to discover: with almost perfect precision,

Supreme Court justices widely viewed as more conservative
are far more likely to be judicial activists than those viewed as
more liberal. Since 1994 the very active Supreme Court declared provisions of sixty-four congressional laws unconstitutional. (By contrast, until 1991, the rate was roughly one every
two years.) Table 5 examines the extent to which each of the
nine judges on the Court agreed with those sixty-four decisions. The table gives as strong an indication as one could en-
vision that conservative judges these days are the true activists
and liberals are the more cautious and circumspect.

We do not know whether the two judges named to the
Supreme Court by George W. Bush will prove to be judicial activists when it comes to overruling the intent of legislatures,
but Samuel Alito's record as a federal judge clearly reveals a
disposition to do so, most noticeably a decision in which he
held (in dissent) that Congress had no right to regulate ma-
chine guns.[16] Everything we know about Judge Alito suggests
that his conservatism is more of the radical than of the conventional kind and that he will be quick to identify with the activism of Justices Scalia and Thomas.

The inevitable consequence of such judicial activism will
be further loss of legitimacy; conservatives can continue to attack liberals for using the Court to advance their agenda, but
now liberals can justifiably attack conservatives for doing the
same thing. The prospects for a nonideological Supreme Court
whose decisions would be considered legitimate by all sides
have rarely been bleaker. Conservatives have, if anything, esca-
lated their attacks on the judiciary, treating courts, just like
they treat the media or the northeastern elite, as hopelessly biased toward liberalism. They demand that Republican presidents exercise far stricter ideological scrutiny over prospective
judges than Gerald Ford did over John Paul Stevens or George

Table 5. Willingness to Override Congressional Provisions, 1994–2005

Judge	Percent of Provisions Overruled
Clarence Thomas	65.63
Anthony Kennedy	64.06
Antonin Scalia	56.25
William Rehnquist	46.88
Sandra Day O'Connor	46.77
David Souter	42.19
John Paul Stevens	39.34
Ruth Bader Ginsburg	39.06
Stephen Breyer	28.13

Source: Paul Gewirtz and Chad Golder, "So Who Are the Activists?" *New York Times,* July 6, 2005.

H. W. Bush did over David Souter. Even judges as reliably conservative as Anthony Kennedy or Sandra Day O'Connor were attacked when they reached decisions that did not stand full square with conservative policy preferences on such issues as gay rights or affirmative action. Tom DeLay and other conservatives denounced judges, including those appointed by Republicans, who did not rule in favor of the parents of Terri Schiavo, the brain-dead woman in Florida. In one of the most chilling statements ever uttered in the U.S. Senate, John Cornyn, a Republican from Texas, said in the wake of the ruling that he could understand why violence against judges had been escalating, seeming by his remarks almost to endorse such violence. Such an atmosphere of intense politicization is difficult to stop once launched, but that does not prevent prominent politicians from launching it.

The consequences that follow when the judiciary becomes polarized could hardly be more serious, for if there is no final court of appeal trusted by all sides in a controversy, that controversy is likely to escalate. Americans, who distrust politicians so deeply, desperately want to trust the judiciary; they were willing to forgive the Supreme Court even when it rendered a partisan decision in *Bush v. Gore*. But that trust is fragile and could be lost. If the judges appointed by President Bush prove themselves to be true conservatives respectful of institutions and appreciative of history, the Court is likely to preserve its legitimacy. Should they instead turn out to be more interested in ideological orthodoxy and partisan results, not only will the Court become a superlegislature, judges will be subject to the same degree of distrust and unpopularity now reserved for congressmen. That is a limbo any self-respecting judge presumably would want to avoid. Yet it will be difficult to avoid, so politicized has the judiciary in America become.

One additional group should be added to the list of those striving for a vantage point of objectivity that might enrich the quality of American political debate. The years after World War II were ones in which academic social scientists began to collect and analyze massive amounts of data. At least some of them saw in the social sciences valuable tools that could improve public policy; social science findings would offer policy makers advice uncolored by the self-interest of lobbying groups or the frequently demagogic rhetoric of political parties.

An especially interesting example of the role social science could play in offering a disinterested voice to government involved those writers who, alarmed at the ideological passions unleashed during the 1960s, decided to publish a new journal that would bring to American life qualities of reason and complex judgment that only immersion in real-life data could offer. "It is the essential peculiarity of ideologies," Daniel Bell and Irving Kristol wrote in the first issue of their magazine, "that they bitterly resist all sensible revision. *The Public Interest* will be animated by a bias against all such prefabrications."[17] At the time, 1965, the only ideologies that mattered, at least in the sense of influencing public policy, were leftist ones, and as a result, *The Public Interest* developed a conservative reputation, even though it did feature articles from time to time by liberal writers. It would be more correct, however, to describe its politics as skeptical rather than conservative, for its main task was never in doubt. Whether dealing with housing, crime, the war on poverty, or health care, the writers who contributed to the magazine demonstrated that good intentions were never enough; social science evidence was often fragmentary and inconclusive, but unless policy planning was accompanied by whatever wisdom it offered, it would probably fail.

Many of the writers who published in *The Public Interest* did not trust liberals to put aside their ideological blinders when confronted with evidence that their favorite policies were unlikely to work. Their suspicions were confirmed when the sociologist James C. Coleman, a *Public Interest* author, wrote a report suggesting that the family backgrounds of inner-city children contributed more to their performance in school than the amount of money spent on the schools. (Coleman would also eventually conclude that busing had failed because, in contributing to white flight, it helped resegregate schools in ways that were detrimental to learning.) In an early manifestation of what would come to be called political correctness, Coleman was vilified for views that ran counter to liberal convictions. For Coleman himself, and for *The Public Interest* writers more generally, the controversy over his work demonstrated the power of objective social science and reinforced their conviction that left-wing ideology was out of touch with empirical reality. Those most harmed by liberal "prefabrications," moreover, were the very people liberals believed they were trying to help; in the controversy over busing, for example, liberals were so convinced of the virtues of integrated schools that they failed to recognize how attached many African-American parents were to their neighborhood schools, even if those schools were segregated.

The Public Interest flourished when liberals were in power; after conservatives came to control so many branches of government, its voice, at first less compelling, was eventually stilled, and it ceased publication in 2005. All this would be understandable, and cause for warranted celebration, if the conservatives who have come to power had decided to take the advice of *The Public Interest* to heart and put aside ideology in favor of hard knowledge, thereby rendering irrelevant the magazine's raison d'être. But this, for the most part, contemporary conservatives never did. In fact, as is also true of their approach to judicial activism, conservatives went well beyond the liberals of the 1960s in substituting ideological inclination for objective data. The mistake of the liberals who formulated public policy during the 1960s was to ignore evidence that contradicted their preconceptions. The goal of conservative policy makers is not to ignore such counterfactual evidence but to suppress it. Attacks on science are by no means the preserve of the political right; leftist postmodernists had little use for the objectivity science requires and the truths it establishes. But on the issue of scientific neutrality, the right's power to challenge the role of science in public life has been far more consequential than the speculations of the academic left. Since at least 1913, when the act establishing the Federal Reserve System began to involve the American government in widespread efforts to collect unbiased data about an important matter of public policy, the United States has never witnessed as direct an assault on the notion that good public policy requires disinterested information as it has in the years since George W. Bush became president.

Conservative preference for ideology over disinterested data was most clearly noticeable on any issue in which religious conservatives have shown great interest. Both the Department of Health and Human Services and the Centers for Disease Control relentlessly pushed "abstinence only" programs, despite a paucity of evidence proving that they work, going so far as to delete from the CDC Web site important information about condom effectiveness.[18] Along similar lines, President Bush, at a January 2005 press conference, cited "studies" which proved that adopted children raised by heterosexual parents do better than those raised by gay parents, even though no such studies exist.[19] The Bush administration's hostility toward social science findings was not restricted to ideologically charged topics, however, but influenced policy making in a wide variety of arenas; a 2002 Department of Education memo, for example, requested the removal of information from the department's Web site of information not in accord with the administration's "philosophy."[20] (This was the same department that had paid the conservative journalist Armstrong Williams $250,000 to promote the administration's agenda.) If conservatives fail to treat justice as disinterested, it can hardly be surprising that they approach social science data the same way. Policy must always guide empirical investigation, not the other way around. There are, from this point of view, no such things as facts. There are only conservative "facts" and liberal ones, and conservative policy makers are interested only in the former, not the latter.

One other important difference between earlier liberal resistance to objective data and contemporary conservative hostility to the same idea must be noted. For all their discomfort with social science findings that undercut cherished orthodoxies, earlier generations of liberal policy makers strongly encouraged public policy to base itself on the findings of natural science, especially with respect to the environment and the regulation of food and drugs. No such regard for objective scientific fact characterizes the Bush administration's approach to these issues. The administration's attempts to politicize science received considerable attention in February 2004, when sixty top scientists, including twenty Nobel Prize winners and previous science advisers to Republican presidents, criticized administration attempts to suppress scientific findings. Besides examples involving birth control, they pointed to efforts by the administration to suppress data about bacteria in the vicinity of hog farms, to downplay and then to drop entirely warnings about global warming, to subject appointments to scientific review boards to political scrutiny, and to ignore scientific advice that ran counter to the administration's insistence that Saddam Hussein possessed weapons of mass destruction. As the journalist Chris Mooney has pointed out, the Republican attack on science bears all the hallmarks of crafted talk and data manipulation associated with the drive to privatize Social Security or the decision to invade Iraq. When conservatives denounce "junk science," or call for fairness in the composition of review boards, or ask for additional studies before considering economic regulations, they are using the language of open inquiry to shut down objective scientific investigation.[21]

Two of the most important political constituencies of the Republican Party fueled this disdain toward objective science.

Corporate interests, especially pharmaceuticals and industries that extract resources from the ground, were worried that objective science might cast their products and procedures in a bad light. And the religious right, hostile to science since at least the days of Scopes trial, had never given up trying to dismiss the theory of evolution. To please both constituencies, the Bush administration did far more than suppress information or distort data; it demanded as well equal time for quasi-scientific research produced by industry or, in the case of intelligent design, developed by faith-oriented think tanks. In many ways, this was the more pernicious development, for scientific research that is suppressed in one place can appear somewhere else. But to treat scientific truth as if it were an opinion to be balanced against other opinions is to undermine science's claim to provide insights that exist on a different level from opinion. It was as if the Fox News model of political shouting had become the appropriate model for treating such issues as global warming, the teaching of biology in high schools, or whether abortions cause breast cancer. Natural science, like social science, became just one more weapon in the ideological war conservatives are fighting; if its results support the conservative side in the war, they are used, but if they do not, they are not.

The United States has come a long way from the days in which a magazine like *The Public Interest* could cast a cold eye on overheated claims and, in so doing, remind all sides in Washington's never-ending battles that there are standards of reason that will remain long after the battles are forgotten. Looking back on the lessons of the Great Society, Lyndon Johnson's ambitious efforts to involve government in a myriad of issues designed to improve the quality of American lives, two writers for *The Public Interest* summarized the magazine's stance

Plight/concerns
among
Citizenry

not
universal

this way. "The social problems requiring remedial action by government are usually complicated," they began. And, because "their causes are not understood in their entirety and the proposed cures are of uncertain efficacy," governmental officials should "proceed with caution in areas where it lacks knowledge and experience, in the expectation that second efforts at social intervention will be improved by what is learned from the initial experiments."[22] The authors were right to advocate realistic policies based on an open and experimental attitude to social reality. What they could not know at the time they wrote was that the true enemies of their appeal to reason would be conservatives seeking to roll back the Great Society, not liberals seeking to defend it. Objective science is one more victim of a political culture that has become so passionate in its pursuit of self-interest that it no longer has much room for the general interest.

America was hardly perfect—it may not have even been better—when its media were monopolized, its establishment firmly in charge, its judges fearful of politics, and its social scientists in search of an objectivity they frequently had difficulty finding. Disinterested elites are a blessing to democracy when they are right, but if they are wrong, their unresponsiveness can easily turn into inflexibility. New Yorkers were treated to an unfortunate case of an elite gone wrong in 1967 and 1968, when McGeorge Bundy, then president of the Ford Foundation, led a campaign to decentralize public schools in Brooklyn's Ocean Hill–Brownsville district; Bundy's effort opened scars barely closed almost forty years later.[23] There is, moreover, a fine line between the wisdom an establishment can offer and the arrogance with which it offers it; patrician self-righteousness can corrode democracy as surely as patrician

self-confidence can nurture it. Debates over the meaning of
the 1960s are likely never to end, but there is little doubting
that the opening up of one institution after another provided
opportunities for women, minorities, and others excluded
under the rules of the old politics of democracy; even conservatives owe their political success to those movements for
openness and access. When disinterest is just another name for
privilege, disinterest loses its appeal.

American democracy is paying a significant price for its
lack of institutions of disinterest. The single most important
political contribution that disinterested groups make to democracy is their ability to call a stop to politics. Consider what
happened to the civil rights issues of the 1960s. The South had
never been known for its willingness to accept national legislation it viewed as interfering with its way of life, and just as it
resisted the victory of the North in the Civil War, its initial reaction to *Brown v. Board of Education* and the Civil Rights Act
of 1964 was to dig in its heels. But *Brown*, the product of a less
contentious era, was decided by a unanimous U.S. Supreme
Court, a seeming impossibility today, while the 1964 act was
passed only with the strong bipartisan support of the Senate
minority leader, Everett Dirksen, again something difficult to
imagine in these more ideological times. (The fact that significant numbers of Republicans voted for the 1964 Civil Rights
Act, and that an equally significant number of Democrats
voted against it, has been all but forgotten.) With the support
of social science research, upon which the Court relied in
Brown, along with a solid commitment to racial equality on
behalf of the unofficial establishment, civil rights was transformed from a contentious ideological issue to a consensus
moral imperative, and with that, resistance to legalized segre-
gation in the South eventually crumbled. By calling an end to

politics, just about every disinterested institution in the United States enabled Americans to put an ugly past behind them and to move forward, however tentatively.

The contrast between the closing off of the politics around civil rights a generation ago and the inability to close off politics around the culture war of today is striking. Poll after poll shows that Americans have little taste for the intense partisanship and ideological extremism surrounding judicial nominations or so-called "hot button" issues like the right to life. Yet in the absence of any authoritative institution capable of calling a stop, a culture war that has lost its purpose continues to spin out of control. As a result all Americans suffer, save those ideological interest groups with a stake in keeping the culture war alive. When passions get out of hand, as they have when a political system has become as divisive as America's is today, someone has to step in and say no. Americans are beginning to witness what happens when no one can effectively do that. Endless cycles of blame and vituperation that resemble a Kentucky blood feud hardly seem an appropriate model for democracy at the start of the twenty-first century, but that is what happens when institutions that stand for trust and dispassion are treated with so little trust and so much passion. Conflictual, hyperactive, emotional, the new politics of democracy tends to exhaust all those who participate in it. And even if we wish to bring the new politics of democracy to an end, we lack the means. Democracy without disinterest means politics without end.

Democratic governing in its ideal sense puts forth policy that strives to benefit those who put into it, citizens but it has become so much more to its [demise] opposite of benefit?

VI
Democracy Without Justice

Elected with the strong backing of the religious right, conservative politicians in the United States frequently talk in the language of morality. Stances that defend the culture of life, uphold chastity, discourage homosexuality, protect children, and promote marital fidelity attract them. They identify international conflicts as struggles between good and evil. By substituting questions of character for matters of policy, they invite voters to judge them on the basis of their virtue. They are comfortable bringing religion into politics and politics into religion. Because of their success, moral issues dominate American politics. Anyone who believes that democratic political systems cannot ignore ultimate questions about the meaning and purpose of life ought to thank organizations associated with the Christian right for raising them in the context of election campaigns and policy debates.

Yet morality is usually thought of as demanding stuff, requiring that we dedicate ourselves to God, or lead a life of virtue, or seek to uphold the common good. Due to such stern imperatives, the introduction of moral questions into politics can easily come at the cost of morality itself. This is not just because those who speak in the language of morality do not always live up to its standards; corruption in Washington did not come to an end when politicians strongly supported by the religious conservatives became the majority party, and one after another right-wing political activist seems to have had problematic sexual affairs or to be involved with such unsavory activities as gambling. Corruption of that sort, however, is not a new story in the United States; nineteenth-century politics had more than its share of graft, and the sexual liaisons of politicians routinely ignore the ideological divide. Hypocrisy is one of the few aspects of American politics that is genuinely bipartisan.

Moral corruption is more serious business. "Morals themselves are liable to all kinds of corruption," Immanuel Kant once wrote, "as long as the guide and supreme norm for correctly estimating them are missing."[1] That supreme norm—the ability to act for the sake of a principle that universalizes our actions—is especially absent when politics concerns itself with one of the most fundamental of all moral goods: justice. The questions of what justice is and how it can be realized have been addressed in myriad ways from the days of Plato and Aristotle to those of John Rawls and Michael Walzer. But underlying nearly all contemporary accounts of justice is the same feature that makes it possible for democratic societies to call an end to politics: disinterest, or, as moral philosophers like to call it, impartiality.[2] Well captured by the Kantian categorical imperative, as well as by Rawls's request that we evaluate the merits of a policy by imagining that we do not know who will benefit from it, justice requires that we act out of a sense of duty to others rather than for comfort and convenience to ourselves. In today's world, an inclination toward justice means assuming an obligation toward others, particularly those to whom life has been unfair, and then doing what is possible to redress the conditions that make it so.

Some degree of injustice will be a fact of life so long as societies exist on this side of utopia. But Americans have begun to experience a rather dramatic shift toward injustice in recent years as income inequality has risen sharply at home and as efforts to protect and extend human rights have come to play a decreasing role in American foreign policy. These trends in the direction of greater inequality are not confined to one political party; as I shall remind the reader in this chapter, Bill Clinton sponsored welfare reform and was less than enthusiastic about responding to clear cases of genocide abroad. For this reason, a trend toward injustice seems to represent something deeper in American political culture than the policy choices of this or that administration. It is nonetheless striking that injustice has become so apparent at the same time that morality is considered so important. How a political system so responsive to the moral concerns of some of its most devout citizens nonetheless managed to decrease the level of justice at home and abroad is a puzzle that future generations of historians and theologians will have to ponder. For now, it is enough to suggest that democracy without justice is a nearly perfect expression of the moral corruption against which Immanuel Kant warned.

"Until about a century and a half ago," the political philosopher Brian Barry has written, "justice was a standard understood as a virtue not of societies but of individuals."[3] Social, as opposed to individual, justice is a distinctive feature of modern societies. So long as justice involves only an individual quest to do good, society itself is under no obligation to protect its most vulnerable members against misfortune. But when justice becomes a social good, it is no longer considered acceptable—indeed it is a source of great shame—if preventable tragedies such as hunger, deprivation, and debilitation are allowed to happen.

To appreciate what it means for society to lack a sense of social justice, one has only to turn to the Social Darwinist ideology that gripped American thinkers toward the end of the nineteenth century. William Graham Sumner, the most famous adherent of this way of thinking, disliked not only government intervention into the economy but even private acts of charity designed to help the poor; only the laws of laissez-faire could help people out of poverty, he argued, and any efforts to ameliorate the market, private or public, would only worsen their condition.[4] Whatever justice meant for Sumner, it did not include an obligation on the part of the more favored social classes to help those born into the least favored ones. Sumner's views about religion were complicated—ordained in the Episcopal Church, he flirted with nonbelief later in life—but never did Christianity convince him that the Sermon on the Mount ought to become the basis for public policy.

No sooner did Sumner begin to articulate his views than opposition to them began to arise. Other Christians were aghast at Sumner's naturalistic indifference to the plight of the least fortunate; in the late nineteenth century, both the Protestant Social Gospel and Catholic encyclicals such as *Rerum Novarum* insisted on ties of mutual obligation that Sumner renounced. Political reformers, some religious and others secular, transformed those ideas into reality first during the Progressive Era and then during the New Deal. Both symbolically and practically, principles of social justice achieved their most important legislative expression with the passage of the Social Security

Act of 1937; in ways that surely would have shocked Sumner, Americans agreed to tax themselves in order to ensure that none of them would face the prospect of old age with no viable means of support. To be sure, the New Deal was imperfect and would in any case run out of energy by the late 1930s.[5] No reformer after Franklin Delano Roosevelt, furthermore, was able to extend the New Deal's concern with social justice to matters of health care. Yet there is no gainsaying the significance of what the New Deal accomplished: it brought Americans into a world in which government would take active steps to combat what Barry calls "morally arbitrary inequalities."[6] Without in any way losing their enthusiasm for capitalism and private property, Americans internalized the most fundamental principle of social justice: the worst that happens to others could perhaps happen to them, and, as a result, everyone should be protected against catastrophe to the most realistic degree possible.

Despite the popularity of the New Deal, American political rhetoric over the course of the past three or four decades has turned against the notion that the poor deserve a fair shake from everyone else. In response to the turmoil unleashed during the 1960s, conservatives found an effective populistic language for questioning the idea of social justice; liberal elites, they claimed, determined to take the side of underclass predators, were out of touch with the inclinations and understandings of ordinary people. Richard Nixon spoke in such terms when he made law and order the theme of his 1968 campaign. So did Ronald Reagan when he denounced "welfare queens" living lives of luxury on governmental handouts. Populism, for all its identification with the average person, is not a movement of the very poor against the very rich; its themes are nearly always evoked to defend the respectable lower middle class against the unearned luxuries of the aristocratic elite on the one side and the presumed slothful self-indulgence of the underclass on the other. Those themes became so firmly lodged in American political culture that Democrats could not resist them; only by promising to end welfare as it had always been known were the Democrats under Bill Clinton able to stave off their vulnerability against Republican attacks on this issue. Especially in contrast to the more ambitious domestic programs of an FDR or an LBJ, Clinton's presidency was characterized by a preference for incremental reform at best.

With the election of George W. Bush, however, an important change took place in domestic politics and policy. Emboldened by their 2004 victory, Republicans no longer prided themselves, as Ronald Reagan had done, as the true inheritors of FDR's legacy. Instead, they set their sights on popular New Deal programs themselves, even those that worked to the benefit of the middle class. By proposing to privatize Social Security, George W. Bush struck at the philosophical heart of the principle of social justice it embodies: the capacity of government to guarantee Americans some financial support in their old age irrespective of the performance of the economy. Other prominent conservatives were even more explicit than the president in their opposition to the New Deal; one of them, Janice Rogers Brown, whom Mr. Bush successfully appointed to the federal bench after a threatened Democratic filibuster was averted, denounced the New Deal as embodying slavery.

Yet attempts to transform the New Deal did not gain as much traction as the conservative politicians who launched them might have anticipated from their successful attacks on welfare; Brown, for example, has so far been passed over for a Supreme Court vacancy, and Social Security reform proved to be a dead letter. In their opposition to New Deal liberalism, conservatives faced one significant obstacle: for all the right-ward political turn evident in America, the notion that social justice is an ideal worth pursuing still remains fairly strong in the minds of most Americans. Because it does, no serious contemporary policy maker or office holder, outside of a few extreme libertarians, would ever rely on the harsh rhetoric of a William Graham Sumner. The fact that conservatives today appeal to compassion, praise private charity, and speak in explicitly religious language suggests, if anything, that they rely on the very means of helping the vulnerable that Sumner once denounced. In their zeal to roll back the reforms of the New Deal, conservatives who appear too callous or indifferent to the needs of ordinary Americans, including the vulnerable and the elderly, are likely to lose whatever political popularity their moral populism has helped them gain.

Republicans ideologically committed to rolling back the New Deal therefore have little choice but to try to accomplish their objective of reducing the level of social justice without attacking the idea of social justice itself. This is a difficult goal to achieve, but those bent on realizing it do have one advantage: the new politics of democracy works in their favor. All of the features that have contributed to declines in the quality of democratic performance reviewed in the previous chapters of this book can be exploited to launch a campaign against social justice without appearing to do so: because people lack some of the basic knowledge about politics they need to make informed decisions, they frequently fail to consider the implication of legislation dealing with tax reform or economic policy more generally; because politicians are anything but indifferent to public's lack of knowledge, they can willingly exploit public ignorance to achieve ideologically driven objectives; because accountability is especially difficult to ascertain under conditions of incumbency protection, legislators need not fear paying an electoral price for decisions that would be unpopular if publicized by challengers intent on taking away their seats; and because political institutions, up to and including government itself, are handicapped by widespread public cynicism concerning their ability to act in the public interest, political leaders have a freer hand to reward the already wealthy and powerful while ignoring the claims of the underrepresented.

No issue better illustrates the ways in which democracy's qualitative shortcomings produce wildly unjust results than the Republican-inspired tax cuts of 2001 and 2003. The unfairness contained in those measures is beyond dispute. The top 1 percent of Americans are slated to receive approximately 40 percent of the benefits of the 2001 tax cut, and this at a time when the incomes of the very rich were rising in any case. Put another way, slightly fewer than 200,000 of the highest-income Americans will receive the same total benefit as 124 million of the lowest-income households in the United States.[7] One estimate of the combined effect of the two tax cuts, furthermore, suggests that in the year 2010 taxes paid by the richest Americans will have declined by 25 percent while the poorest Americans will have seen a cut of only 10 percent.[8] This is the Rawlsian difference principle turned upside down: the greatest advantage goes to the most well-off. It is as if advocates for the tax cut took a seminar offering readings from every serious theorist of social justice in the West and then decided to pursue a policy directly opposite to what they would have urged.

From the standpoint of theories of justice, it matters little whether programs that cause significant injustice are popular, even among those who are treated most unfairly; popularity and morality are not the same thing. Yet Mr. Bush's plan to cut taxes did not, in fact, enjoy especially wide support. To be sure,

Americans did approve of the Bush tax cuts, sometimes by large majorities, but as few as 5 percent of Americans believed that issues involving taxation were among the nation's most serious problems, and Americans generally insist that the very rich pay less than their proper share of the tax burden.[9] Americans are not nearly as accepting of high tax rates as citizens of other countries, but nor do they think that taxes should be cut if doing so means that budgets will be unbalanced or that popular programs such as Social Security and Medicare will be jeopardized.[10] Taken as a whole, public opinion created no demand for tax cutting and remained ambivalent about the idea even when the administration made it the centerpiece of its political agenda.

The key factor that enabled the Bush tax cuts to pass was not public support but public ignorance. One might assume that Americans would be familiar with the basic facts of tax policy, since their own pocketbooks are affected by congressional legislation. This, however, turns out not to be the case. A 2003 survey supported by National Public Radio, the Kaiser Family Foundation, and the Kennedy School at Harvard shows just how little attention the American public pays to such matters. The summary of its findings offered by Larry Bartels is worth quoting at length:

> Asked whether they pay more in federal income tax or Social Security and Medicare tax, 34 percent of respondents said they didn't know (and most of the rest were wrong). Asked whether they were eligible for the Earned Income Tax Credit, 28 percent said they didn't know. Asked whether Americans pay more or less of their income in taxes than Western Europeans, 42 percent said they didn't know. Asked

whether they had heard about a proposal in Washington to do away with taxes on corporate dividends—the centerpiece of President Bush's new
tax proposal and a prominent feature of political
debate in the month before the survey—61 percent
said no. Asked whether the 2001 tax cuts should be
sped up, 48 percent said they didn't know. Asked
whether the cuts should be made permanent rather
than being allowed to expire in 2011, 60 percent said
they didn't know. Asked whether speeding up the
cuts and making them permanent would mainly
help high-income, middle-income, or lower-income
people, 41 percent said they didn't know. Asked
whether "most families have to pay the federal estate tax when someone dies or only a few families
have to pay it," half of the respondents mistakenly
said that "most families have to pay," while an additional 18 percent said they didn't know. And more
than two-thirds of those who favored repealing the
inheritance tax endorsed as a reason for doing so
that "It might affect you someday"—a wildly optimistic assessment for all but the very wealthiest
survey respondents.[11]

Bartels's research has been criticized by other political
scientists who argue that at least Republican supporters of the
tax cuts were quite aware of their reasons for supporting it;
they believed that future economic growth produced by the
cuts would ultimately enrich the public treasury.[12] Still, even if
their findings are correct, they apply only to some Americans
and they suggest less that these Republicans were informed
than that they knew enough to repeat the prominent talking

points of their party without critically examining them. (No reputable studies have ever shown that cutting taxes actually raises governmental revenue.) In that sense, they add a corrective to Bartels's larger point, but they do not undermine the main contention: Mr. Bush's tax cuts were accompanied, at the level of public opinion, with considerable ignorance and wishful thinking.

Such an atmosphere allows considerable scope for political elites to fashion policies as they see fit. The resulting flexibility could lead to policies that are more just than public opinion supports; were liberals in power under such conditions, they could rely on widespread public ignorance to push for taxes more progressive than Americans might like. But liberals are not in power under the new politics of democracy; conservatives are. And they can use the very same flexibility to adopt programs far less just than the public believes justified. Conservatives know what they want. The public has little idea what it wants. Under such circumstances, unjust actions are easier to undertake because a public that admires justice in the abstract has little notion that it is supporting injustice in the concrete.

A political system in which politicians are held accountable for the consequences of their actions might mitigate such seemingly irrational effects, but as it currently operates, the American political system does not do a good job holding policy makers to their word. Accountability is expected to operate roughly like a mandate: the electorate feels that a problem is serious and deserves attention; politicians offer competing proposals to deal with their concerns; the politicians whose proposals most accord with the public's desires win; and then policies are proposed along the lines promised. Nothing resembling such a process took place around the 2001 and 2003 tax cuts, in large measure because so many of the congressmen who voted for it faced no meaningful electoral opposition within their districts. And because increasing numbers of congressional districts are homogenous in class composition, politicians representing better-off ones have even less incentive to do anything on behalf of the less well-off.

In the absence of accountability, moreover, political leaders, up to and including the president, are under no obligation to offer justifications for their proposals that meet even elementary tests of consistency or accord with any known empirical realities. Not only was there little demand for the Bush tax cuts, the justification offered for a new policy, as was also true with Social Security privatization and the war in Iraq, changed as the policy itself remained steadfastly fixed. Originally offered as a way to return the government's surplus to the citizens to whom President Bush claimed it rightfully belonged, tax cuts later came to be justified to bring to the United States sufficient economic growth to restore the very surplus that had disappeared on Mr. Bush's watch. Low criteria of accountability even allowed Republicans to expand governmental spending significantly as they cut taxes radically, as if the input side of government had no relationship at all with the output side.

So many different, even contradictory, rationales for the economic benefits of cutting taxes could be offered because the real objective of the cuts had little or nothing to do with the economy; their purpose was to restrict the ability of government to pursue social justice by eliminating the money that would enable it to do so. No wonder, then, that obfuscation played such an important role in the passage of both tax cuts. The president consistently claimed that the biggest rewards of the tax cuts would go to the least well-off; statistics were manipulated to give an incorrect impression of who would benefit and who would not; and the long-term costs of the program were hidden by making the tax cuts temporary under the reasoning that, once they became entitlement, no future politicians would restore taxes no matter how large future deficits became. If the Bush tax cuts were *not* symbolic of rising public support for injustice, they *were* symbolic of the increasing moral corruption of American politics. A policy that the majority of Americans did not especially want was passed by means of which they would not approve.

In a just political world, such an outcome would not be acceptable. But Americans have been told so frequently that justice is impossible or impractical because everyone is always motivated by self-interest that they have become relatively willing to allow injustice on such a massive scale to take place behind their backs. Government, the one institution capable of acting impartially, is treated by them with such overwhelming cynicism that government rarely does act impartially. Given their skepticism toward politics, Americans would at first probably be shocked to learn how blatantly unfair is the distribution of benefits under the tax cuts of 2001 and 2003, but once they recovered, they would quickly conclude that such unfairness is the way politics always happens. Policy makers intent on furthering injustice can count on such cynicism just as they can take advantage of widespread ignorance. In so doing, they may conform to the negative image Americans have of them, but so long as American negativity lacks any real bite, those who use their public positions to reward the rich and powerful rarely pay a political price for their acts.

Tax policy, as it happens, offers only one example, albeit a huge one, of the ways in which the procedural imperfections of the new politics of democracy allow right-wing ideologists to pursue unjust policies. Three months before President Bush signed the tax cut of 2001, Congress passed and sent to the president for his signature a law nullifying a rule from the Occupational Safety and Health Administration that offered workers protection against ergonomic injuries in the workplace. Ten years in the making, the OSHA rule, designed to give workers some protection against employers, had widespread public support; employers, especially those in highly competitive industries, wanted it modified, but for just about everyone else, the issue had been settled. But the affected industries that wanted the rule changed, empowered by their campaign contributions, as well as the politicians eager to take their money, knew that they could achieve their objective when the public was not paying much attention. Working outside the limelight, and relying on legislative rules that bypassed committee hearings, reviews, and filibusters, both houses of Congress, in the course of one week, rushed through a bill killing the rule.[13] It may be true that fair procedures would never have allowed so unfair an outcome, but unfair procedures work together so well with unfair outcomes that everyone with a stake in injustice could take advantage of them.

Committed to leaving no stone unturned, the Bush administration was remarkably thorough in its campaign to overcome decades of relatively just public policies. The environmental regulations of the Clinton-Gore years were quickly overturned to please mining and forestry interests. Pharmaceutical companies won protection against the ability of large drug purchasers to negotiate lower prices. Regulatory agencies took the already established practice of siding with the industries they regulate to new levels. In perhaps the most stunning example of its instinct to give a higher priority to business than the concerns of ordinary Americans, the Bush administration, always so quick to evoke the fear of terror, saw no reason to oppose a takeover of the management of a series of American ports by a company controlled by the United Arab Emirates. The policies were too uniform and widespread to be happenstance. George W. Bush and his Republican allies came to power with a decided preference for inequality; a determination, missing in the more genial years of the Reagan administration, to bring its unjust vision of the world to fruition; and a willingness to take advantage of flaws in the democratic system to get results.

Given the remarkable redistribution of income and power during the Bush years away from those who need wealth most in favor of those who need it least, it would be tempting to conclude that we are witnessing a return to the days of William Graham Sumner. But this is not correct. Sumner, after all, was a Social *Darwinist*. Inherent in his outlook on the world was the notion that injustice is a fact of nature; markets have evolved through a process of natural selection—in his view, all the more reason to denounce as hopeless directed human action to shift social outcomes one way or another. Injustice was a prominent feature of Sumner's worldview, but it was passive injustice, the kind that leads us to believe that the San Francisco earthquake or Hurricane Katrina is unjust; we can be sympathetic to the victims, but we are not responsible for what happened to them. The most appropriate criticism of Sumner's perspective is that he urged Americans not to take action when taking action could have helped reduce injustice.

Contemporary Republican politics is guided by another view of injustice entirely. They are not sitting back indifferently as nature takes its course; on the contrary, they are using the human and social techniques at their command to bring about even higher levels of inequality. The difficulties the victims of their policies will face making ends meet are not the result of God-given acts beyond human intervention but matters for which those responsible could, in a more just world, be held accountable. Indeed, to make the world more unjust, the architects of today's conservatism must acknowledge, and meet head-on through distortion and manipulation, the widespread commitments to social justice that surround them; they cannot hide behind the excuse that injustice is inevitable because justice is impossible. They are in that sense not spectators to injustice but active participants in its creation. Shunning rhetorically Sumner's indifference to injustice, their actual policies are even more unjust than those of the heyday of Social Darwinism, for we know now, even if we did not fully appreciate the fact then, that no society need live with such high levels of social injustice if it chooses not to.

It is one of the supreme ironies of contemporary politics that the only force capable of preventing the Bush administration from creating even more socially induced injustice was a natural disaster. By reminding Americans of the degree of poverty in their midst, Hurricane Katrina did what Democrats had not been able to do; they stopped, at least for a time, Republican efforts to repeal the estate tax, make permanent the 2001 and 2003 cuts, and take even further steps to increase the already high levels of inequality in the United States. Yet as if to prove one more time that contemporary injustice is a product of human decisions rather than acts of God or nature, Republican conservatives resumed their determination to make the world a more unfair place as soon as public attention to the effects of Hurricane Katrina began to wane. Searching for ways to protect the Bush tax cuts while protecting themselves against charges of fiscal irresponsibility, congressional Republicans proposed radical cuts in public programs relied upon by the poor. Meanwhile, contracts to Republican campaign contributors for rebuilding the devastated areas were handed out without competitive bidding, and plans were revived for "free-enterprise zones," designed to allow market forces to work. To be sure, President Bush's plans to suspend minimum wage laws in hurricane reconstruction were blocked, but with that exception, Republicans were steadfast in their determination not to allow a natural disaster to influence their decided preference for policies that help those most who need help least.

The political scientists Paul Pierson and Jacob Hacker have argued that the Bush administration has torn up the books that used to be written about political strategy; no longer is it necessary to appeal to the center if one has a strong enough ideological base.[14] Along the way, Republican politicians are rewriting the rules of democracy, taking advantage of every weapon in their arsenal to reward friends and punish what used to be called (quaintly, it now seems) the loyal opposition. In one further arena of public life are contemporary conservatives radicals in disguise: without ever coming clean about their intentions, they are trying to re-create a nineteenth-century political system in which justice is a virtue of individuals rather than a goal of society. Taking advantage of people's trust in their leaders and indifference toward policy to achieve such a breathtaking result requires remarkable political skill, and for that, Republicans are to be congratulated. But let no one call it moral. By the standards of justice that have long existed in the United States, the Bush tax cuts and efforts to gut workplace and environmental regulations, along with the corruption of the democratic process required to achieve such objectives, are among the more immoral actions taken by any presidential administration in the past century.

If principles of social justice within the United States are only a hundred years old, those on behalf of international justice are behind by a half a century. It was not until the end of World War II that the international community—through the Nuremberg principles of 1946, the Genocide Convention of 1948, and the Universal Declaration of Human Rights adopted by the United Nations General Assembly, also in 1948—agreed on a set of norms based upon standards of human rights. At a time when the war on terror takes priority for so many Americans, and with it claims to protect national security by any means necessary, it is easy to pass over these remarkable postwar accomplishments. The legal scholar Mary Ann Glendon gets it correct when she writes that the Declaration of Human Rights "joins ideas associated with liberty-based constitutionalism to a strong commitment to social justice," and that working together, these principles embody "a vision of ordered liberty grounded in an understanding of human beings as both individual and social."[15]

International norms of social justice, unlike domestic ones, never achieved anything like consensus in the United States, even in the years in which they were formulated. In January 1949 the president of the American Bar Association denounced the Universal Declaration of Human Rights on the grounds that it would "promote state socialism, if not communism, throughout the world."[16] That kind of language became a staple of the isolationist and anticommunist sentiment that gripped the United States in the decades after World War II. Standing in the way of an American commitment to international norms of social justice was the force of American nationalism. As Anatol Lieven has argued, Americans and Europeans came away learning different lessons from the catastrophe known as World War II. Europeans understood their twentieth-century history as proof of the dangers into which nationalism could lead and wanted to see created a world order that would allow for international cooperation. Americans, by contrast, adopted the very nationalism that Europe was abandoning. In the wake of the twentieth century's experiences with totalitarianism, the United States could no longer afford isolationism. But its involvement with the world borrowed from the isolationist tradition the conviction that the world outside America's borders was hostile and corrupt. The United States can and should involve itself with foreign countries, this form of nationalism acknowledged, but only if the process was under American control.[17]

When it comes to foreign policy, populism is nationalism's first cousin. The enemies of the American nation, populists tirelessly assert, are the elitists of the East Coast establishment. Whether they are depicted as wealthy Wall Street lawyers or dedicated communists hardly matters; they are what the conservative activist Phyllis Schlafly calls the "supersophisticates," the cultured, semiaristocratic, globalists who love Europe more than they admire the United States.[18] From a populistic perspective, human rights, global social justice, and humanitarian aid are exactly the kinds of issues that preoccupy elites; ordinary people themselves know that the only sure way to defend the country is by spending considerable sums on weapons and showing a willingness to use them. Such views are not always accurate; Americans actually responded positively to President Jimmy Carter's efforts to emphasize human rights, and they have been particularly interested in the fate of Christians in non-Christian countries and noncommunists in communist ones. According to the reputable Chicago Council of Foreign Affairs polls, moreover, Americans support even such controversial human rights measures as the International Criminal Court.[19]

But there is also considerable truth in the populistic claim. When conservative populists launch attacks on domestic social justice, they frequently fail; when they launch them against

efforts to promote social justice around the world, they generally succeed. American support for global idealism is too dif-
fuse, and enemies of human rights in Congress and the military
are too strong, to resist the emotionally powerful combination
of nationalism and populism which insists that the United
States should always treat humanitarian ventures with suspicion. Populism is in its own way responsive to considerations
of social justice domestically, but it is never sympathetic to the
same considerations internationally.

Once identified with the extreme right, populistic suspicion of foreign policy elitism is now commonplace in American politics. In part, the reason lies in the failures brought about
by the foreign policy elite itself, especially in Vietnam. But they
also lie in the greater democratization of American public life
that occurred in the aftermath of the 1960s and 1970s. The
same forces that made it impossible for political parties to be
run by unelected bosses or that demanded greater public access to corporations and universities also made it difficult for
an aloof foreign policy elite to decide what was in the national
interest and to count on the widespread public trust to ratify
its freedom of action. The United States has tried many approaches to foreign policy over the course of its history, but the
ones that are especially resonant in populistic times are neither
a Hamiltonian globalism nor a Wilsonian humanitarianism,
but a Jeffersonian distrust of the world and a Jacksonian insistence on national honor.[20]

The great advantage of populistic foreign policy making
is that Americans are unlikely to give their support to a war
that takes huge numbers of American lives for reasons difficult
to articulate. (The war in Iraq shares futility with Vietnam but
not the number of American casualties.) The single biggest
shortcoming of a populistic foreign policy is that relatively un-

popular actions that nonetheless do good in the world—especially those involving considerations of global social justice—are harder to realize. Populistic wariness toward international idealism helps explain why it was not until 1986 that the U.S. Senate ratified the Genocide Convention (and why another two years had to pass before the legislation was implemented); why it took until 1992 for the U.N.'s International Covenant on Civil and Political Rights to be approved; and why the International Covenant on Economic, Social, and Cultural Rights was never ratified. Once a leader in proclaiming the vital importance of global human rights, the United States quickly became a laggard.

America's resistance to considerations of global social justice takes many forms, including its relatively low contributions to developmental assistance; its protection of domestic industries, despite its frequent calls for free trade, even when such protectionism harms Third World manufacturing; its suspicions toward the United Nations; its hostility toward such international environmental treaties as the Kyoto Protocol on global warming; its support for regimes such as those in Saudi Arabia that deny fundamental rights to their own citizens; and its religiously driven lack of interest in family planning. But the most striking example of its indifference to justice abroad—one, alas, that it shares with Europe—has been its unwillingness to take action against genocide. In the past three decades, situations that appeared to be genocidal under the definition contained in the Genocide Convention developed in Cambodia, Iraq, Rwanda, the Sudan, and former Yugoslavia, yet only in the last of these did the United States take effective action against it, and even those actions generated fierce resistance in Congress. "Genocide," as Samantha Power has written, "has occurred *after* the Cold War; *after* the growth of human rights groups; *after* the advent of technology that allowed for instant communication; *after* the erection of the Holocaust Museum on the Mall in Washington, D.C."[21] As Power writes, political leaders rarely take action against genocide unless they feel political pressure to do so, but such political pressure is highly unlikely to occur without political leadership. In a populistic political culture, neither the supply of nor the demand for such leadership exists.

In response to the horrific genocides of the 1990s, governments around the world negotiated the establishment of an International Criminal Court in 1998. Its purpose was not only to reiterate that genocidal actions were in violation of international law but to create a tribunal with authority to try those who committed genocidal acts against their own people. A month before leaving office, President Clinton signed the treaty, but at the same time, he recommended that Congress defer ratification pending resolution of American objections. Clinton was concerned that attempts would be made by the ICC to try Americans; this possible violation of American sovereignty was simply a nonstarter in America's increasingly populistic political culture. The ICC treaty has been approved by sufficient numbers of countries to take effect, even though it still lacks American support. The covert hostility toward international social justice in the aftermath of World War II had become, fifty years later, sufficiently overt to influence Democrats as well as Republicans.

Because American commitments to issues involving international justice have been so weak—and so bipartisan in their weakness—one might conclude that relatively little space existed for the Bush administration to weaken them any further. Yet such a conclusion fails to recognize the determination of contemporary conservatives to reject what they believe to

be the misguided idealism that brought about the U.N. Declaration of Human Rights and the Genocide Convention in the
first place. As a candidate in 2000 George W. Bush had questioned "nation building" as a U.S. strategic objective, making
clear his plans to break with the already feeble efforts of the
Clinton administration to intervene abroad in the name of
justice; as his future national security adviser Condoleezza
Rice put the matter, U.S. military forces are "most certainly not
designed to build a civilian society."[22] Of course, this is precisely what the United States eventually found itself doing in
Iraq, but this was because its reliance on military force to en-
gineer regime change in that country had failed. Still, even
when it found itself engaged in nation building, the Bush administration went about the task by relying on its own military
and by rejecting international cooperation. Its unilateralism
was never in doubt; in 2001 it pulled out of any American involvement in the Kyoto global warming treaty, and one year
later, not content merely to allow the International Criminal
Court treaty to die a slow death in Congress, the administration took the unprecedented step of withdrawing the American signature and then began cutting foreign aid to any country that refused to sign agreements offering immunity to any
Americans who might be brought before the court.

In taking steps such as these, the Bush administration was
sending a signal that it was not going to pay much, if any, attention to considerations of global social justice. By themselves,
the rejection of Kyoto and the ICC were not unexpected; nearly
all postwar governments, Democratic or Republican, were suspicious of treaties that could, however dubiously, be viewed as
detracting from American sovereignty. Just carrying forward
the inclinations of previous administrations, however, was not
sufficient for the activists of the Bush administration; they

wanted to put their own mark on global social justice, and they did. Just as in domestic policy they moved from passive to active injustice, in foreign policy they decided not only to look the other way when injustice took place but to practice some injustice of their own. For reasons never presented to the public, the Bush administration responded to the events of September 11, 2001, by accepting the necessity for torture as an instrument of American statecraft. Instead of insisting that the world hold itself to a higher standard, the administration concluded that it would reduce itself to the lowest.

That American troops relied on torture at the Abu Ghraib prison in Iraq is beyond dispute.[23] But Abu Ghraib is only the tip of the torture iceberg: torture was used at the U.S. base in Guantánamo, Americans "rendered" detainees to countries such as Syria with terrible records of human rights, and the CIA operated illegal torture prisons in at least two eastern European countries. While denying that it ever engaged in torture, the Bush administration has been determined to protect the president's authority to use it. Even after an effort led by Senator John McCain resulted in the passage of language that banned cruel and degrading treatment of prisoners in American custody, President Bush, upon signing the bill that contained the McCain Amendment, issued a statement indicating that he would not be bound by its language. For all its denials, the Bush administration made little secret of the pride it takes in responding to terror threats with tough measures, whether they include actions that violate the Geneva Accords or have historically been associated more with dictatorships than with democracies. For President Bush, and even more vehemently for Vice President Cheney, human rights were from Venus, while brutal treatment of prisoners was from Mars.

How did a society that has long stood for individual freedom and opposition to totalitarianism come to endorse the explicit use of torture? It seems clear that the same kinds of imperfections in democratic performance that allow policy makers to cut back on domestic commitments to social justice without appearing to do so also allow them to reverse course on human rights policy while still claiming a mission to spread democracy and freedom throughout the world. If democracy is understood to be a political system in which leaders are held accountable to the views of an informed public, American democracy has rarely if ever functioned well in wartime. Congress, the most democratic branch of government, refrains from proclaiming wars. Presidents invariably ask for powers during war—declared or not—that render their actions less accountable. Opposition parties, knowing that they will be accused of lacking patriotic zeal, frequently do not try to block the president. All these developments have important implications for international social justice. It is difficult even under the best of circumstances to win public support for intervention against genocide or to promote efforts to improve the lot of the world's most disadvantaged people. In times of war, it is close to impossible. War is understood to be a threat to the state, and the state has little choice but to protect itself until the war is over.

The Bush administration's singular contribution to the tense relationship between war and democracy has been to launch a war that, for all intents and purposes, will never be over. Because terror will never cease, human rights need never advance. Under George W. Bush, the United States has reached the point where not only is the promotion of justice abroad ignored while a deliberate reliance on injustice is proclaimed necessary; any efforts to return to more normal conditions are to be placed outside consideration of what is deemed to be in

the interests of the United States. If the assumptions underlying the war on terrorism are taken seriously—and President
Bush has gone out of his way to reject any attempt, even ones
by his own administration, to change either the terminology
or the designated goals of the engagement—the United States
will never again be able to claim that it is capable simultaneously of protecting its national security and making the world
a fairer and a better place. The global consensus around social
justice that the United States helped solidify in the aftermath
of World War II actually remains rather powerful; institutions
are in place to try genocidal leaders, and standards exist that
make it impossible for those leaders to claim national sovereignty as a shield for their actions. Alas, however, the United
States itself is no longer part of this international consensus.
American politics has its priorities, and global social justice is
not one of them.

Democracies ought to promote justice; built into their political DNA, so to speak, is opposition to the exercise of arbitrary
political power and respect for the equality and dignity of all
citizens.[24] Yet democracies are not, in the words of the political
philosopher Richard Arneson, "intrinsically just"; their procedures may be fairer than those of autocratic political systems,
but majorities are quite capable of lining up behind policies
that fail to serve just ends.[25] It is not only that democratic societies frequently act unfairly in the way they distribute government's resources; democracy is poorly structured to achieve
the position of impartiality that justice so frequently requires.
Political leaders rarely make good Kantians. It is not their job
to tell lobbyists that what benefits them most ought to be resisted precisely because they gain from it. Nor would Americans expect their political leaders, in the spirit of Kant, to judge

the actions of nations in the world, especially including their own nation, on the basis of a universal point of view. Any legislator who evaluated an appropriations bill on the basis of the good it realized for society as a whole or who put international standards ahead of the American national interest would be quickly voted out of office by constituents more concerned with benefits for their community and country than with decisions taken behind a veil of ignorance. Democracy achieves just outcomes only by working against the grain of democratic expectations.

Of all forms that democracy might take, moreover, populistic democracy is especially unlikely to act from a morally just point of view. Populism is fueled by the conviction that people know what they want and are entitled to get it—a reasonable enough sentiment in political terms, but one that rarely factors into its decision making reflection, dispassion, duty, impersonality, compassion, obligation, or any other quality generally associated with strong conceptions of justice. Populism operates by appealing to people's most basic, even sometimes most primitive, emotions, not by concluding, as Rawls's difference principle would command, that it provide the greatest advantage to the least well-off. The more populistic American politics becomes, the less likely it will be to resist the impatience of those who seek personal gratification, the redress of moral grievances, and the satisfaction of national honor through political means.

American politics has shifted in a radically more populistic direction with the advent of the new politics of democracy. The costs and benefits associated with this shift will be judged differently by different individuals, but it is hard to avoid the conclusion that among the most serious costs of this new way of doing public business is the active promotion of injustice both at home and abroad. A world governed by a just God has a punishment for injustice: the sinful will be denied salvation. A well-functioning democratic political system containing strong notions of accountability also has the capacity to punish injustice: those who violate the fundamental moral values for which the society stands will be voted out of office the next time citizens have a chance to express themselves. Even the market, albeit with a bit of government regulation, can police injustice, so long as those who practice it are exposed in ways that allow consumers to boycott their products. The world is never perfectly fair, and injustice will always exist. But human beings have been able to deal with the injustice of the world around them by establishing theological, political, and economic institutions and practices that seek to repair the damage that injustice renders to society's moral fabric.

No such sense of closure is available under the rules of the new politics of democracy. How tempting the conditions of contemporary American politics must be to anyone determined to make life for the rich and powerful more comfortable at the expense of the poor and vulnerable. Counting on the trust of voters who know little about the policies they advocate, they can use their control over government to manipulate information to their advantage. Unconcerned about electoral competition, they need not fear that the unjust actions they take will be subject to the scrutiny of opposition research. Aghast at the idea that impartiality is either possible or desirable, they are quite capable of putting into place rules that work to their advantage and prevent public exposure of what they are really doing. And, in their most daring act of all, they can even claim while doing all this that they hold the moral high ground, for they are the ones, they insist, who represent the party of moral values and religious scruples. This is immorality squared. Not only would the United States do terrible things, it would use terrible means to deflect responsibility and hide the consequences of its acts.

Conservatives have, in their quest to make the world a more unjust place, no doubt learned one thing: the only effective check on their power is that their own consciences might inform them that what they are doing is wrong. But they also know that this will never stand in their way; for all their talk of the sincerity of their faith, they are people who have never given any indication of being constrained by conscience. The new politics of democracy has offered them a golden opportunity to prove that life is not only unfair but can be made even more unfair by their actions, and this is an opportunity they are not going to pass up. Unfortunately, at least morally speaking, they will leave behind a society far more coarse, indifferent, corrupt, and ugly than the one they inherited from the liberals they so frequently denounce for their immorality.

opinion that
has a lot of
basis in
empirical data

VII

The Rise of Conservative Democracy

Political science, alas, is not a science along the lines of biology or physics; the number of propositions it has uncovered which are accepted across the board as true is astonishingly small. Still, American political scientists have given considerable attention to questions of how and how often Americans vote, whether they hold their leaders accountable, how cynical they are toward parties and interest groups, what their leaders do with the power vested in them, and how those leaders try to build support for the policies they propose. The overwhelming evidence they have produced suggests that when it comes to matters of quality control, American democracy is not functioning well. Democracy increasingly takes place without—or without enough—information, accountability, institutions, disinterest, and justice.

In examining the causes and consequences of these problems, there is plenty of blame to spread around. Bill Clinton was a master of the art of using the public's lack of interest in policy to promote the policies he favored. Democrats relied upon their control of Congress to enhance their power in the past just as Republicans do today. The trends that have weakened political parties as agencies of mobilization produced candidate-centered politicians—whether named Jimmy Carter or Ronald Reagan—intent on running against Washington. All administrations engage in efforts to spin the media to their side. Questions of social justice were so widely ignored in the Bush-Cheney years because so little attention had been paid to them in the Clinton-Gore years. The background factors that have contributed to the rise of the new politics of democracy—the culture war on the one hand and an increasing reliance on populistic language and programs on the other—cross all partisan and ideological lines.

At the same time, however, attempts to blame both parties equally for the sorry state of American democracy ignore two indisputable facts. The first is that Republicans have had far more power than Democrats in very recent American political history; whether or not they continue to control all branches of government after 2006, their dominance has enabled them to transform the political system in directions they favor. The second is that Republicans practice the arts of the new politics of democracy better than Democrats: they are (or at least have been) more united, more focused, more determined, more successful. Politics operates not in some ideal world but in the here and now, and in the here and now of the new politics of democracy, Republicans have played the game as superbly as Democrats have been bumbling and uncertain. Democracy is not unlike sports, and Republicans, in recent years, rank as Super Bowl champs.

If Republicans deserve disproportionate credit for winning under the new rules of American politics, they must at the same time accept major responsibility for the damage their victories have caused. Voter ignorance, autocratic policy making, partisan division, self-interested lobbying, unjust policies—none of these is new in American public life. But many of the ways in which the Republican majority used its power in the early years of the twenty-first century are, to say the least, unusual, including the virtual exclusion of the opposition party in the House from any legislative or investigatory role; a willingness to allow private interests affected by proposed legislation to write the bills that concern them; a policy of imposing partisan loyalty tests on scientists and other ostensibly nonpartisan experts in the administrative branch of government; a reliance on dubious, if not downright false, data to achieve policy outcomes; the hiring of friendly journalists to propagandize in favor of proposed policies; claims of executive power that, if taken at face value, essentially eliminate the need for the two other branches of government; foreign policy making by advisers close to the vice president and secretary of defense that ran roughshod over the expertise provided by area specialists; a pronounced tendency, noted by nearly every policy maker who left the Bush administration and then wrote about it, to twist policy to serve partisan ends; reliance upon distortions of the military records of those who questioned the administration's policies; and a determination to fill the judiciary with individuals committed to a distinct ideological viewpoint even while denying that they have any ideological viewpoint whatsoever. Some of these tactics take to their logical conclusion hard-nosed rules of politics that have always existed, while others are literally unprecedented. The combined effect of all of them suggests that new rules about democracy are being written every day. It is as much a compliment to the abilities of Republicans as it is a criticism of their methods to claim that what is called conservatism today has distinct elements of what was called radicalism yesterday.

The political strategist in me admires what Republicans have accomplished. The liberal democrat in me worries about how they have done so. Despite some of the apocalyptic language one sometimes hears on the left, democracy is not about to disappear from the United States, not even in the age of Bush and Cheney.[1] But liberal democracy is democracy of a very particular and fragile kind, one that not only respects the will of the people but protects fairness, disperses power, and encourages pluralism. Neither the culture war nor populism matches up well with liberalism, and all too often the party that benefits most from both of them, the Republican Party, disdains not only the liberalism of the Democrats but the broader kind of liberalism that cherishes open and responsive government. Does American democracy still work? Of course it does. But does it work with sufficient respect for the liberalism that has enabled Americans to live up to their founding ideals? That is the more difficult question to answer.

The term "liberal democracy" is used so frequently that we commonly assume that the adjective must come along with the noun. Yet as the journalist Fareed Zakaria has pointed out, one need not always accompany the other; societies such as Russia or India have in recent years become more democratic, but they are also decidedly illiberal. Opposition parties find it difficult, if not impossible, to challenge heavily entrenched regimes. Religious passion fuels frequently violent conflict and encourages intolerance. The media are carefully controlled. The judiciary serves the state more than it delivers justice. There is such a thing as illiberal democracy, Zakaria concludes, and it may be growing. "In countries not grounded in constitutional liberalism, the rise of democracy often brings with it hypernationalism and war-mongering."[2] Certainly recent attempts to democratize the Middle East support Zakaria's contention; Hamas in Palestine and the Muslim Brotherhood in Egypt may be popular, but no one would call them liberal.

The United States *is* grounded in constitutional liberalism, and its politics, as a result, have little in common with what is occurring in societies that were dictatorships not long ago. Still, the question needs to be asked: what exactly does the "liberal" mean in liberal democracy? Surely it should not mean liberal the way the Democratic Party is characterized as liberal; one can disagree with domestic reforms based on the principles of the New Deal—or, in more current usage, one can be against affirmative action or gay marriage—and still be an adherent of liberal democracy. Being a liberal democrat does not carry with it an ideological stance on the world; there are people on the left end of the political spectrum who are as hostile to both liberty and democracy as is anyone on the right.

If it is wrong to view the liberalism of liberal democracy as a political ideology, it is not incorrect to point out that philosophical liberalism adheres to certain assumptions about human nature or the use of power that have their origins in the thought of John Locke and Adam Smith.[3] Liberalism in this more capacious sense of the term makes a virtue of tolerance and, by so doing, tends to be suspicious of anyone who claims divine sanction for religious truth. Whether embodied in an eighteenth-century preference for economic laissez-faire (today's defining conservative idea) or a twenty-first-century concern with civil liberty (a preoccupation of contemporary leftists), liberalism has always questioned the unchecked centralization of political power. Expressed in such forms as Immanuel Kant's notion of "perpetual peace" or by commitments to international law, liberalism has historically been distrustful of war and the mobilization of state power, and to the appeals to nationalistic emotion it brings in its wake. Liberalism, finally, has long been intertwined with a commitment to reason; those in positions of power cannot simply cite matters of state as the basis of their actions but must justify their decisions based on widely accepted legal, moral, and, in some cases, scientific standards. By marrying this capacious philosophical understanding of liberalism to the expansion of the franchise that began in the nineteenth century, liberal democracy created a political system based on majority rule, but also one in which the majority came to appreciate the importance of limited government, individualism, the rule of law, respect for empirical reality, and pluralism in ideas and institutions.

It has recently become fashionable, both on the right and on the left, to criticize liberalism by deconstructing its claims to neutrality or by trying to show that it relies as much on violence as the ideologies against which it contrasts itself. Liberalism, we are told by such critics as Alasdair MacIntyre and Stanley Fish, can never be neutral between Enlightenment and pre-Enlightenment outlooks on the world because it is inextricably linked to the former.[4] With respect to the United States, these critics are correct; America's framers were strongly influenced by ideals of reason and science.[5] Between different contemporary political positions—whether health care should be provided by the market or the state, whether conservation or exploring new sources is the best way to deal with the high cost of energy—philosophical liberalism has no policy preferences. But between different sets of ideas that have historically been dominant in the West, the "liberal" in liberal democracy *is* partisan: it is *not* on the side of those who insist that because everything is interpretation, no truths can be assumed; or that because there is no universal morality, the protection of human rights is little more than an attempt to impose an ideological worldview on those who do not share it; or that because the existence of God cannot be proven one way or the other, science and religion constitute equally valid (or invalid) guides to public policy.

Liberal societies do have their limitations; they pay relatively little attention to community, offer insufficient respect for tradition, and frequently fail to take full account of the obligations one generation owes another. But their virtues are otherwise palpable. When domestic conflicts are treated as resolvable through compromise, passions are restrained, extremism contained, and violence tempered. Those who respect others with whom they strongly disagree tend to receive respect in return. If public life is tame, private life can flourish. Moderation in politics makes progress possible, ensuring that not every political disagreement becomes a fight over first principles. Individualism allows speech to be heard, art to be created, science to innovate, business to expand, and faith to flourish; indeed strong belief is far more possible in a liberal political system than liberalism is in a theocratic one. Turn-taking permits stable government over time, as the party in power at one moment understands that it might be in opposition at another. Social justice is possible because everyone can put himself or herself in the place of anyone else. Liberal societies are more inclined to live in peace with each other, but when peace breaks down, unified more by the common desires of all its citizens than by despotic rule, they are quite capable of defending themselves against external enemies. The sociologist Norbert Elias has described modernity as a "civilizing process."[6] Liberal politics can be characterized the same way. Liberalism civilizes the rough and tumble of democratic politics, making it possible for people with very different conceptions of the good society to share the common benefits of citizenship.

Because liberalism in the philosophical sense is more inclusive than liberalism in the political sense, many of those who call themselves conservatives share a taste for civilizing politics. Their goals are to promote stability, and their means are to encourage moderation. Cognizant of their country's history and respectful of its traditions, they want to restore the balance between freedom and order more in the direction of the latter, even if they would not mind seeing business have more of the former. Worried about insurgencies and threats to world order, they seek to build up American military power as the best way of ensuring peace. This form of conservatism appreciates the occasional need for bipartisan cooperation and shuns radical nihilism, even if it comes from the right rather than from the left. Sentiments such as these characterize the views of a number of prominent Republican politicians and conservative activists, ranging from former Senator John Danforth of Missouri to the journalist Andrew Sullivan to the *New York Times* columnist David Brooks. Any well-functioning liberal polity is enriched to the extent it contains conservatives of this sort.

The movement that propelled the Republican Party of George W. Bush to power in 2000 and 2004, by contrast, was fueled by a different kind of conservative temperament. Frequently associated with the Christian right, this kind of conservatism has turned its back on the Enlightenment and the worldviews that accompanied it. The most conspicuous manifestation of the Christian right's unease with the Enlightenment can be found in its rejection of modern science, especially Darwinism. But more important for the future of liberal democracy is the unease with the modern ideal of civil politics that pervades the ideas and actions of large numbers of right-wing politicians and activists, not all of whom are associated with, or even speak for, the Christian right. Listen to such talk radio hosts as Rush Limbaugh, the former Republican presidential advisers Oliver North and G. Gordon Liddy, the syndicated columnist Ann Coulter, and an unseemly number of Republican congressmen and senators and you hear not the respectful conservatism of an Edmund Burke, whose fear of radicalism was tied to a distinctive liberal temperament, but the vituperative anger of reactionary haters of modernity such as the German thinker Carl Schmitt.

Tolerance, for one thing, is not among the virtues whose absence in modern America these extremist voices lament. They engage in no-holds-barred styles of attack in which considerations of fairness are dismissed as naïve or unaffordable. Insistent on the importance of morality, they have no taste either for social justice or for the impartiality upon which it has so frequently been based. Neither reasoning nor reasons ever change their minds. To rally their supporters to their cause, they rely not on argument but on the arousal of fear—the easiest, although also the most frustration-inducing, of emotions. Political debate is not a search for common ground but a forum for the constant reiteration of agreed-upon talking points. Opposition parties are not potential partners in governing the country but enemies of the country to be excluded from power and policy. Science does not establish facts about the natural world that permit public policy to move forward but provides a cover for the antireligious bigotry these commentators attribute to their opponents. If it bothers them that a country conceived in liberty engages in torture, they do not say so. They call for a return to the traditional values, and they do so by appealing to a form of traditional politics that, in its passion, bellicosity, and intransigence, more resembles a duel designed to reclaim honor than negotiation and compromise designed to temper extremism.

Even America's most conservative zealots do not poison their opponents in election campaigns, shut down opposition newspapers, or suspend elections when they fear they may lose them; their views, in that sense, cannot be equated with the "illiberal democrats" described by Fareed Zakaria. (It does not help their claims for respectability, though, when one of them, the Rev. Pat Robertson, calls for the assassination of a foreign head of state or informs those who choose to teach evolutionary biology that, having abandoned God, they will surely be abandoned by God.) At the same time, the hard-right activists who serve the contemporary Republican Party can hardly be called liberal democrats in the mold of John Stuart Mill or John Rawls. Some other term is needed to characterize their views. I will call them conservative democrats, but understood in a particular way. What best characterizes their worldview is not political conservatism—if anything, they are quite radical—but the kind of disposition which believes that liberal political systems are too optimistic about human nature, too afraid to acknowledge the brutal need for violence, too committed to the false idea that neutrality in politics in both desirable and necessary, and too unwilling to take whatever steps are necessary to protect themselves against enemies abroad and at home. Conservative democracy is a political system based on majority rule, which makes it democratic. But it also flourishes without Enlightenment-inspired commitments to fairness, impartiality, tolerance, and reason, which is what makes it conservative.

The democratic side of conservative democracy cannot be emphasized enough; no one forces huge numbers of Americans to listen to Rush Limbaugh, and even the most extreme right-wing politicians in Washington were duly chosen by voters in their districts. As much as the rise of the conservative right shows the vibrancy of democracy, however, it also demonstrates the vulnerability of liberalism. None of America's three branches of government has been immune to its ugly and destructive kind of politics, and all have suffered as a result.

Conservative democracy has made its greatest inroads in the U.S. House of Representatives. As the research of the political scientist Elizabeth Anne Oldmixon has shown, the introduction of moral and cultural issues into the legislative process encourages members of the House to take extreme positions on which negotiation and compromise become difficult or impossible.[7] This—combined with incumbency protection, increasing partisanship, a near-complete absence of debate, and one-party governance without minority participation—marks a sharp break with liberal assumptions about how conflicts should be resolved and the public's best interest considered. It is one thing for virulent extremism and intolerance of dissent to dominate the airwaves and another thing entirely for them to characterize the leadership of a legislative body. Intent on winning, whatever the cost, House leaders have acted as if winners have nothing to fear and losers nothing to remember. Politics being what it is, they may someday find themselves out of power. If they do, their voices will be heard and views considered only if the liberals they denounce now act as real liberals then.

Matters are not nearly so desperate in the Senate, where traditions of civility and bipartisan cooperation continue to exist. Yet the Senate came perilously close to eliminating its liberal procedures in 2005, when Republicans threatened to invoke the appropriately named "nuclear option" to foreclose the right of Democrats to filibuster against judicial nominees they considered too extreme. Ultimately the nuclear option was avoided; senators from both parties were able to fashion a compromise that preserved Senate traditions, and President Bush nominated candidates for the Supreme Court well enough qualified, and sufficiently skilled at never revealing their actual views, to avoid a filibuster. Still, it is a cause for some concern that Senate Majority Leader Bill Frist showed so little respect for the institution over which he presided when he endorsed the nuclear option and had to be constrained by a revolt from the ranks. Nor does it inspire confidence that an increasing number of senators are recent arrivals from the more ideological House and lack an appreciation of the Senate's history and traditions. Reviewing the events of 2005, including the threat of the nuclear option, the historian Lewis Gould concluded that "the Senate had become more often an impediment to democratic government rather than a place to express sober second thoughts on national priorities." The decline of the Senate's independence particularly concerned him: "The Framers of the Constitution envisioned a Senate that would function as a judicious check on both executive power and the House of Representatives. They did not imagine a body that would act as a rubber stamp for an incumbent president."[8]

The issue that came close to tearing the Senate apart—the selection of judges to federal courts—involved the second branch of government, the judiciary. As if to reflect the polarizing character of contemporary American politics, the U.S. Supreme Court has for some time rendered nearly all of its major decisions by a 5–4 majority, with Justice O'Connor frequently providing the deciding vote. This stands in sharp contrast to the situation a half-century ago; *Brown v. Board of Education,* for example, the 1954 decision that outlawed segregated schools, was decided by a unanimous court. One of the many reasons why compromise decisions seem so difficult to obtain on today's Supreme Court is that so few of its members, unlike those of the Warren Court, which decided Brown, served as elected politicians. (O'Connor, the great compromiser, not surprisingly did; she had been elected to the Arizona State Senate.) In theory, politicians ought to be partisan and judges impartial; in practice, the exact opposite has been true. By replacing O'Connor and Rehnquist with judges known primarily for ruling from the bench, John Roberts and Samuel Alito, President Bush not only found conservatives; he continued a trend of selecting individuals for the Court with little experience in the give-and-take of real politics. This is likely to continue a pattern in which the Court reinforces the ideological battles so visible in the other branches of the U.S. government rather than serves as an alternative to them, especially given the fact that Alito, the more ideological of the two, was chosen to replace the far more moderate O'Connor. If the Court were to overturn any of its recent 5–4 precedents, and if it were to do so by voting 5–4 in the other direction, its political and ideological mission, already displayed in the *Bush v. Gore* decision, would stand out even more sharply than its judicial sensibility.

And then there is the third branch of government, the executive. George W. Bush has been the most ideological politician ever to hold the office of president of the United States. Whatever his theory of leadership involves, it has not included respect for opposition parties and acceptance of a pluralism of viewpoints. President Bush's chief political adviser, Karl Rove, has practiced politics as if it really does represent war by other means.[9] He has used innuendo to smear his opponents. He has interpreted even the narrowest of victories as complete vindication. In his conquest and use of power, all is permitted, even that which by tradition is forbidden. There is no way of knowing whether Rove, the living embodiment of conservative democracy, has discovered new laws of political behavior or has been the beneficiary of circumstances (including luck) unlikely to be repeated in the future. But to the degree that Rove's tactics have worked—they did, after all, result in two victories for George W. Bush—they will serve as models for future candidates intent on winning at all costs. The one law that Rove's success inevitably confirms is Gresham's: in the currency of political campaigning, the bad will be driving out the good for some time to come.

Karl Rove has not only advised George W. Bush in electoral campaigns, he has played an active role in governance, and the Bush style of using power has been as illiberal as the Bush method of gaining power. President Bush was never able to separate his position as leader of the United States from his role as leader of the Republican Party. He could have responded to the September 11 attack by unifying the country; instead, he chose to build a stronger Republican majority. Many of his legislative initiatives—tort reform, limitations on public sector unions, a new Medicare law—were designed to weaken or to attract constituencies that habitually vote for Democrats. The nightmare of Iraq played out with domestic political considerations in mind; George W. Bush was as quick to charge Democrats with disloyalty for objecting to the war as he was to cite their support to avoid taking responsibility for it. In the Bush-Rove view of the world, the Democratic Party is not an opposition party that can be expected to take over the reins of government in the future. It is instead viewed as an enemy camp to which no olive branches are to be offered or concessions to be made. So regal has been President Bush's theory of governance that even members of his own party were treated with disdain when they dared challenge him over such issues as banning torture, engaging in unsupervised wiretapping, and entering into contracts with foreign-owned firms to manage U.S. port security. When executive authority is wielded with so little concern for responsibility and accountability as it has been under George W. Bush, the entire liberal infrastructure of politics is threatened.

As these examples from all branches of government suggest, the Republican victories of 2000 and 2004 created a right-wing majority determined not only to pass legislation it favored but to transform the liberal understandings of how politics ought to work that have guided the United States since the eighteenth century. Americans, as a result, are witnessing politics without civility, and the sight is anything but pretty. Take away the restraints liberalism imposes on the conquest and use of power, and all that is left is power itself, to be used in any way those who hold it feel they can. Quick to praise the wisdom of ordinary Americans while denouncing Europeans for their arrogance and elitism, Republican conservatives have brought to these shores not only a European-style authoritarianism in governance but the extremism and vitriol that usually accompany it.

If right-wing politicians have every right to try to push America away from liberal policies and toward conservative ones, they have no right to try to substitute conservative democracy for liberal democracy. Such breathtaking adventurism can be achieved only by stealth, bad faith, irresponsibility, contempt for history and tradition, and the conviction that dedication to ideology trumps love of country. After the disputed election of 2000, there took place a debate in the United States over whether George Bush had been ever granted a mandate to pursue conservative policies. But even if one ac-

cepts that he did have such a mandate, one that was strengthened by his reelection in 2004, no one ever elected him and the
Republican members of Congress to rewrite the rules of how
American democracy ought to function. Yet they carefully studied all the imperfections that have emerged in the new politics
of democracy—voter ignorance, weak conceptions of accountability, poorly functioning intermediate institutions, pervasive
distrust that undermines commitments to neutrality, and fears
of violence that weaken commitments to social justice—and
rolled them together in a sustained, and frequently brilliant,
campaign to instantiate conservative democracy, to bring about
an America that Americans would not recognize, and certainly
would not want. The biggest question facing American politics
in the future is whether their efforts will be brought to their
logical conclusion.

Fortunately, the triumph of conservative democracy is anything but inevitable. The one thing conservative democracy
cannot offer, and the one thing Americans may well decide
they crave, is stability. Moral and cultural controversies and
the ubiquity of populistic politics are not healthy for the liberalism in liberal democracy. At the same time, they promote in-
stabilities serious enough to lead many Americans to believe
that liberalism, and the stability it promises, may not be not
such a bad thing after all.

   Form and function, for one thing, clash in the new politics of democracy, as conservatives attempt to achieve their
goals in a political system designed by liberals. Separation of
powers, an independent judiciary, free speech, federalism—all
these structural and constitutional elements of the American
political system encourage pluralism and insist on moderation; they are premised on the assumption that no one person,

faction, or interest is ever in possession of absolute truth and that, even if some were, a political system works best by preventing them from realizing it. Considerable irony exists in the fact that so many right-wing politicians and judges insist on absolute adherence to the intent of the constitutional framers, given that those framers created a constitutional system suspicious of absolutist claims on truth as well as on power. If the United States were somehow to revert to the originalism that conservative legal scholars venerate, it would be incapable of completing the moral transformation they advocate.

That moral transformation is totalistic in both design and execution. Those who believe that abortion is murder or homosexuality a sin cannot allow some states to move one way and others another, permit judges leeway in applying the laws, or rely on bipartisan negotiation to discover workable compromises. In demanding that political institutions perform tasks once reserved for religious institutions charged with the salvation of souls, they can brook no dissent and tolerate no equivocation. The tension such voices bring to liberal democracy is never ending. Caught between its liberal rules and its conservative expectations, the new politics of democracy is inherently unstable. If America wants to continue to fight its culture wars indefinitely, liberal democracy will eventually transform itself into conservative democracy, for only then could one side or the other win. If it wants to keep the liberalism bequeathed to it by its founders, it will have to find a way to transcend its culture wars by returning to the by-now old-fashioned liberal idea that because politics is not the same as war, limits must be found before differences destroy.

A further source of instability in American politics stems from the contradictions inherent in conservative democracy itself. Conservatives want to limit popular participation in politics on economic matters; populists want to expand it on moral ones. But this is a division of political labor impossible to maintain. Cut taxes and shrink government, as conservatives demand, and you cannot use government to finance the public's call for moral policing. Praise the wisdom of ordinary people, as populists so frequently do these days, and you cannot call them selfish for wanting all the goods that government can provide, including better insurance in old age, public assistance after natural disasters, and regular increases and stability in their Social Security payments, none of which is compatible with tax cutting and downsizing. Were contemporary conservatives purely elitist, they could please their contributor base; were they purely populistic, they could please their political base. But because they are simultaneously both, they act like Calvin Coolidge in opposing the notion that government should have money while they copy Lyndon Johnson in insisting that it should spend it.

Predictions are always difficult in politics, but this one seems safe: there is no way to pursue policies of expansion and contraction forever. The moment conservative democrats are forced to choose whether their sympathies lie primarily with Adam Smith or John Maynard Keynes, difficulties begin to arise. Those difficulties emerged front and center during the second term of the Bush administration. Stunned by the determination of their party's own president to spend lavishly, but unwilling to consider at any point rescinding their tax cuts, conservatives in Congress either denied that there was any fat to cut out of the budget or began to target programs aimed primarily at the poor and vulnerable. Either choice turned out to be problematic. Conservative attempts to cut programs, even those for the poor, render them politically vulnerable; Americans dislike government in theory but embrace it, often with considerable enthusiasm, in practice. Populistic efforts to resist cuts in public programs, or even to expand them to finance wars or the effects of natural disasters, not only are fiscally irresponsible if accompanied by no plans to increase taxes, they cannot be achieved without considerable demagoguery. Small-government conservatism is not very appealing, but it at least possesses a certain intellectual coherence. Big-government populism wins more votes, yet at the cost of an intellectual incoherence so dramatic that reality is proudly filtered out of its worldview.

The blending of conservatism and democracy is a toxic brew, too toxic for Americans to accept for long. The conservatism to which it appeals can never be spelled out in detail, for if Americans actually saw what it meant, they would repudiate it in an instant. The democracy that allows it to flourish never satisfies; if new government programs work, the public wants more of them, while if they fail, the public wants new ones. Because it is so difficult to be conservative and democratic at the same time, the politics of conservative democracy is the politics of fantasy, a doomed effort to return the United States to the nineteenth century while dealing with the complexities of the twenty-first.

Unable to offer a politics of peace, conservative democracy also cannot promise a politics of privacy. Conservative democrats politicize everything, or at least everything they can: religion is about not a personal spiritual search but an affirmation of policy positions; family life becomes part of a national crusade to restore traditional values; natural disasters are brought on by gay rights or the availability of abortion; American foreign policy is designed to convert the world to our way of life, not to bring about peace or stability. Contemporary conservatism distrusts government as much as it venerates politics. Having inherited from the left the democratizing energies of the 1960s, it too believes that the personal is the political. In a world dominated by conservative populists, even the question of when a feeding tube should be removed from a brain-dead individual is made a matter of partisan debate and congressional intervention. Americans elect conservatives because they tire of liberalism's call for great ambition, only to discover that conservatives call not only for perpetual anger and resentment but for a government as intrusive as it is unwelcome.

Philosophical conservatism in the United States is so weak because practical conservatism is so strong. In the aftermath of September 11, 2001, Americans were responsive to the notion that everything about their society had to change. But as that event recedes in memory, their traditional conservatism sets in; they want normality and a return to business as usual. This is precisely what conservative democrats cannot offer. All they can promise instead is crisis and firmness, and as much as Americans want the latter, if they are convinced that they are facing the former, when they no longer feel a sense of crisis, firmness strikes them as inappropriate and out of touch. The polarizing and hysteria-driven tone of America's culture war has never struck deep roots in the minds of ordinary Americans, and as they turn their attention to the price of oil, the inability of their wages to keep up with increasing prices, the inability of their government to prepare and respond to a hurricane, the prospect of an endless and unwinnable war abroad, signs of corruption and arrogance on the part of those who promised to restore order and tranquility, and clear risks to national security brought about by those who laid special

claim to protect them against terrorism, they just might conclude that liberalism, even if they perceive it as elitist, is prefer-
able to conservatism, even as they acknowledge it is democratic.

Americans already experienced one bout of right-wing enthusiasm during the days of Newt Gingrich's "Contract with
America," and they reacted against not only it but the attempt
by the Republican Party to impeach and convict a duly elected
president. Evidently, however, their reaction was insufficient to
stave off yet another conservative effort at instability. From the
moment that chads began to hang from Florida ballots in the
disputed election of 2000, Americans have been living in a
time of frenzy, as if partisan discipline, one-party rule, ideological extremism, government-sponsored agitprop, and the
priority of politics over law and policy—all relatively rare in
twentieth-century U.S. politics—had become as American as
apple pie. Americans themselves may be apathetic, if not downright cynical, toward politics, but their leaders, especially their
recently elected conservative leaders, treat politics as brinkmanship and find themselves at the brink too often for anyone's comfort.

American politics runs in cycles, and it soon may experience another one. In perhaps the strongest testimony to that
possibility, Newt Gingrich himself came to the conclusion
that Republicans are unlikely to benefit further from the Rov-
ian strategy of mobilizing the base on moral issues and had
better begin trying to appeal to centrists and moderates on
their presumed competence to govern.[10] It is impossible to
know whether his party will follow Gingrich's advice; anger
among grassroots Republican activists may remain too strong
for any leader of the party to ignore it. But the mere fact that a
Republican as prominent as Gingrich was willing to challenge

a way of doing politics that had become so central to his party's success suggests that the era of the new politics of democracy may be reaching its culmination. Were Republicans to abandon the new politics of democracy by nominating a more centrist presidential candidate in 2008 such as Arizona Senator John McCain, there is always the possibility that the Democrats would adopt it by choosing a candidate from the far left; neither culture war issues nor populism has been absent from that party's history. But Democrats, especially with respect to presidential elections, have also learned that victory is impossible for them unless their candidates move to the center in search of independents; the base of left-wing voters is so much smaller and so less passionate than the base of right-wing voters that Democrats have no other choice.

Americans, in short, may eventually tire of the new politics of democracy. Fed up with vituperation, polarization, and endless domestic warfare, they may return to their traditional ideological centrism and begin to look for leaders capable of bringing them together rather than tearing them apart. I, for one, hope they do. Americans deserve to feel better both about themselves and about their society.

But it is clear that any turn away from the new politics of democracy will be a difficult one to achieve. Americans need to think more, not about which political party will best represent them but about the nature of politics itself, what they expect of it and what it expects of them. It is not a revitalized Democratic or Republican Party they need but a revitalized democracy, one charged with restoring the liberalism that conservative democracy has abandoned. Americans must look with a more critical eye at what their country experienced during the heyday of the new politics of democracy—and then they must reject the new politics of democracy as unworthy of them and their country.

To accomplish this objective, both ordinary Americans and their leaders will have to stop their destructive codependence. Real democracy demands not only that the people be praised, but that they be challenged; flattery is the great enemy of good democracy everywhere, a cheap political trick that in the guise of complimenting ordinary people expresses nothing but contempt for their intelligence. Conservative democracy achieves its support by appealing to base forms of emotion and knowledge, leaving Americans frustrated and angry when their leaders, by responding so much to what they say, are unable to give them what they need. In the guise of turning power back to the people, it oversees the growth of a lobbying industry better financed, more powerful, and closer to the needs of special interests than the cozy business-labor cooperation that had characterized the 1960s and 1970s. For all its talk of the God-given wisdom of ordinary folk, it elects whoever happens to be the latest scion of a tiny number of its most aristocratic families. Attacks on government enable large numbers of Americans to vent their anger on politicians, but the politicians who attack government the most are always those who preside over its unrestrained growth. Perfectionist yet cynical, quick to act on symbols while slow to respond with substance, more capable of expressing outrage than of engaging in accomplishment, divisive at home while dismissive abroad, the new politics of democracy offers a recipe not for satisfaction and stability but for the disillusionment that nearly always occurs when people are promised results that cannot be delivered.

Americans will know that their democracy is on the road to recovery when their leaders take them seriously enough to pose difficult choices, provide disquieting information, challenge their assumptions, and elevate their sights. But ordinary Americans too must take a hand in strengthening a form of government that speaks, after all, in their name. There is no avoiding the responsibilities that democracies place in the hands of ordinary people. When they inform themselves about what is happening in the world around them; vote frequently and do so with intelligence; insist that their leaders tell them the truth even when it contradicts their desires; hold their leaders accountable for what they say and do; and show the world that the democracy they have inherited from the eighteenth century is worth protecting and perfecting in the twenty-first— then, and only then, will they be able to claim that they are living up to the honor that democratic citizenship confers upon them. The new politics of democracy appeals to the people. It is time for the people to repeal the new politics of democracy.

Republican party not necessarily for smaller govt overall, but ~ mask their use this to quest for less govt on social issues

Notes

Chapter 1.
The New Politics of Democracy

1. My terminology is indebted to E. Pendleton Herring's *The Politics of Democracy* (New York: Norton, 1965 [1940]), although his use of the terminology is different from mine.

2. E. E. Schattschneider, *The Semi-Sovereign People: A Realist's View of Democracy in America* (Hindsale, Ill.: Dryden, 1975 [1960]), 7.

3. The most informed writer on these topics is Robert Dahl; see especially *How Democratic Is the American Constitution?* (New Haven: Yale University Press, 2001).

4. For some recent examples of this traditional criticism of democracy, see Loren J. Samons, *What's Wrong with Democracy: From Athenian Practice to American Worship* (Berkeley: University of California Press, 2004); John Lukacs, *Democracy and Populism: Fear and Hatred* (New Haven: Yale University Press, 2005); and Roger Scruton, "Limits to Democracy," *New Criterion* 24 (January 2006), 20–28.

5. The strongest case along these lines was made by J. L. Talmon, *The Origins of Totalitarian Democracy* (New York: Praeger, 1960).

6. This has not deterred at least some on the left from believing that it is still possible to put together a winning coalition along the lines of the old politics of democracy; see John B. Judis and Ruy Teixeria, *The Emerging Democratic Majority* (New York: Scribner, 2002).

7. Dahl, *How Democratic*, 154.

8. http://www.harrisinteractive.com/harris_poll/index.asp?PID=285.

9. I elaborate on this point in James Davison Hunter and Alan Wolfe, *Is There a Culture War in America?* (Washington, D.C.: Brookings Institution, 2006).

10. George Lakoff, *Don't Think of an Elephant! Know Your Values and Frame the Debate: The Essential Guide for Progressives* (White River Junction, Vt.: Chelsea Green, 2004).

11. For arguments on behalf of this strong conception of presidential power, see John Yoo, *The Powers of War and Peace: The Constitution and Foreign Affairs After 9/11* (Chicago: University of Chicago Press, 2005), and Christopher S. Yoo, Steven G. Calabresi, and Anthony Colangelo, "The Unitary Executive in the Modern Era, 1945–2001," law.vanderbilt.edu/faculty/pubs/yoo-unitaryexecinmodernera.pdf.

12. On this point, see Anne Norton, *Leo Strauss and the Politics of American Empire* (New Haven: Yale University Press, 2004).

13. John L. Allen, Jr., *All the Pope's Men: The Inside Story of How the Vatican Really Works* (New York: Doubleday, 2004), 122.

14. Alexander Keyssar, *The Right to Vote: The Contested History of Democracy in the United States* (New York: Basic, 2000), 256.

15. Rick Perlstein, *Before the Storm: Barry Goldwater and the Unmaking of the American Consensus* (New York: Hill and Wang, 2002); Lisa McGirr, *Suburban Warriors: The Origins of the New American Right* (Princeton: Princeton University Press, 2002).

16. Michael Kazin, *A Godly Hero: The Life of William Jennings Bryan* (New York: Knopf, 2006).

17. Frank Furedi, "From Europe to America: The Populist Moment has Arrived," http://www.spiked-online.com/Printable/0000000CABCA.htm.

18. Anatol Lieven, *America Right or Wrong: An Anatomy of American Nationalism* (New York: Oxford University Press, 2004).

19. Keyssar, *Right to Vote,* 320.

20. J. M. Balkin, "Populism and Progressivism as Constitutional Categories," 104 *Yale L.J.* 1935 (1995). Available at http://www.yale.edu/lawweb/jbalkin/articles/popprog1.htm.

Chapter 2.
Democracy Without Information

1. V. O. Key, *The Responsible Electorate: Rationality in Presidential Voting, 1936–1960* (Cambridge: Harvard University Press, 1966); Samuel L. Popkin, *The Reasoning Voter: Communication and Persuasion in Presidential Campaigns,* 2nd ed. (Chicago: University of Chicago Press, 1994); Benjamin I.

Page and Robert Y. Shapiro, *The Rational Public: Fifty Years of Trends in Americans' Policy Preferences* (Chicago: University of Chicago Press, 1992); Morris P. Fiorina, *Retrospective Voting in American National Elections* (New Haven: Yale University Press, 1981).

2. Mark J. Hetherington, *Why Trust Matters: Declining Political Trust and the Demise of American Liberalism* (Princeton: Princeton University Press, 2005), 29.

3. http://www.findlaw.com/survey/SCsurveyresults.html.

4. Linda Feldman, "The Impact of Bush Linking 9/11 and Iraq," *Christian Science Monitor*, March 14, 2003.

5. Samuel L. Popkin and Michael A. Dimock, "Knowledge, Trust, and International Reasoning," in Arthur Lupia, Mathew D. McCubbins, and Samuel L. Popkin, eds., *Elements of Reason: Cognition, Choice, and the Bounds of Rationality* (Cambridge: Cambridge University Press, 2000), 214–238.

6. Fiorina, *Retrospective Voting*, 5. Emphasis in the original.

7. Christopher H. Achen and Larry M. Bartels, "Musical Chairs: Pocketbook Voting and the Limits of Democratic Accountability," prepared for presentation at the annual meeting of the American Political Science Association, Chicago, September 1–5, 2004.

8. "Blind Retrospection: Electoral Responses to Drought, Flu, and Shark Attacks," prepared for presentation at the annual meeting of the American Political Science Association, August 28–September 1, 2002.

9. Page and Shapiro, *Rational Public*, 12.

10. Michael J. Graetz and Ian Shapiro, *Death by a Thousand Cuts: The Fight over Taxing Inherited Wealth* (Princeton: Princeton University Press, 2005), 6. See also Larry M. Bartels, "Homer Gets a Tax Cut: Inequality and Public Policy in the American Mind," *Perspectives on Politics* 3 (March 2005), 15–31.

11. Martin Gillens, "Political Ignorance and Collective Policy Preferences," *American Political Science Review* 95 (June 2001), 379–396; Larry M. Bartels, "Uninformed Votes: Information Effects in Presidential Elections," *American Journal of Political Science* 40 (February 1996), 194–230. For a different conclusion, see Richard R. Lau and David P. Redlawsk, "Voting Correctly," *American Political Science Review* 92 (September 1997), 585–598.

12. George F. Bishop, *The Illusion of Public Opinion: Fact and Artifact in American Public Opinion Polls* (Lanham, Md.: Rowman and Littlefield, 2005), 28.

13. Popkin, *Reasoning Voter*, 8.

14. This paragraph is based on the comprehensive analysis of polling data contained in Morris P. Fiorina, with Samuel J. Abrams and Jeremy C. Pope, *Culture War? The Myth of a Polarized America* (New York: Longman, 2005), 34–54.

15. Lawrence R. Jacobs and Robert Y. Shapiro, *Politicians Don't Pander: Political Manipulation and the Loss of Democratic Responsiveness* (Chicago: University of Chicago Press, 2000), 50.

16. Cited ibid., 109.

17. Ibid., 51.

18. John R. Hibbing and Elizabeth Theiss-Morse, *Stealth Democracy: Americans' Beliefs About How Government Should Work* (Cambridge: Cambridge University Press, 2002), 21.

19. Paul M. Sniderman, Louk Hagendoorn, and Markus Prior, "The Banality of Extremism: Exploratory Studies in Political Persuasion," paper presented at the annual meeting of the Midwest Political Science Association, 2000, cited in Hibbing and Theiss-Morse, *Stealth Democracy,* 31.

20. A summary of the procedure is contained in Bruce Ackerman and James S. Fishkin, *Deliberation Day* (New Haven: Yale University Press, 2004), 7.

21. Michael X. Delli Carpini and Scott Keeter, *What Americans Know About Politics and Why It Matters* (New Haven: Yale University Press, 1996).

22. On political awareness among American youth see Karl T. Kurtz, Alan Rosenthal, and Cliff Zukin, "Citizenship: A Challenge for All Generations," National Conference of State Legislators, http://www.ncsl.org/public/trust/citizenship.pdf. I am also indebted to William A. Galston, "Political Knowledge, Political Engagement, and Civic Education," unpublished paper, University of Maryland. On newspaper readership see Delli Carpini and Keeter, *What Americans Know,* 144–145. On talk radio and negative campaigning see David G. Barker, "Rushed Decisions: Political Talk Radio and Vote Choice, 1994–1996, *Journal of Politics* 61 (May 1999), 527–539.

23. Jacobs and Shapiro, *Politicians Don't Pander,* 319–320.

24. These figures come from Stephen J. Farnsworth, *Political Support in a Frustrated America* (Westport, Conn.: Praeger, 2003), 29, 30.

25. Hetherington, *Why Trust Matters,* 31.

26. Farnsworth, *Political Support,* 37–42.

27. Hibbing and Theiss-Morse, *Stealth Democracy,* 3.

28. See especially, Alan Wolfe, *One Nation, After All: How Middle-class Americans Really Think About God, Country, Family, Racism, Welfare, Immigration, Homosexuality, Work, the Right, the Left, and Each Other* (New York: Viking, 1998).

Chapter 3.
Democracy Without Accountability

1. For a recent treatment of Schumpeter's importance, see Ian Shapiro, *The State of Democratic Theory* (Princeton: Princeton University Press, 2003), 50–103.

2. Joseph Schumpeter, *Capitalism, Socialism, and Democracy*, 3rd ed. (New York: Harper Torchbooks, 1962), 264.

3. Ibid., 285.

4. Alexander Hamilton, James Madison, and John Jay, *The Federalist*, ed. Terence Ball (Cambridge: Cambridge University Press, 2003), 256 (no. 52), 302 (no. 62).

5. Julian Zelizer, *On Capitol Hill: The Struggle to Reform Congress and Its Consequences, 1948–2000* (Cambridge: Cambridge University Press, 2004).

6. See David Mayhew, *Congress: The Electoral Connection* (New Haven: Yale University Press, 1974), 13–77. A more recent examination of the impact of some of these factors can be found in Walter J. Stone, L. Sandy Maisel, and Cherie D. Maestas, "Quality Counts: Extending the Strategic Model of Incumbent Deterrence," *American Journal of Political Science* 48 (July 2004), 479–485.

7. Robert Biersack, Paul S. Herrnson, and Clyde Wilcox, *After the Revolution: PACs, Lobbies, and the Republican Revolution* (Boston: Allyn and Bacon, 1999).

8. Gary C. Cox and Jonathan N. Katz, *Eldridge Gerry's Salamander: The Electoral Consequences of the Reapportionment Revolution* (New York: Cambridge University Press, 2002).

9. Ed Kilgore, "The Fix Is In," *Blueprint Magazine*, May 31, 2005.

10. John M. Carey, Richard G. Niemi, and Lynda W. Powell, "Incumbency and the Probability of Reelection in State Legislatures," *Journal of Politics* 62 (August 2000), 671–700.

11. For the 8 percent figure, see Gary C. Jacobson, *The Politics of Congressional Elections*, 6th ed. (New York: Pearson, Longman, 2004), 28; for the 10 percent estimate, see Stephen Ansolabehre and James M. Snyder, Jr., "Using Term Limits to Estimate Incumbency Advantage When Officeholders Retire Strategically," *Legislative Studies Quarterly* 29 (November 2004), 487–515.

12. The 70 percent figure comes from John R. Hibbing and Elizabeth Theiss-Morse, *Stealth Democracy: Americans' Beliefs About How Government Should Work* (New York: Cambridge University Press, 2002), 108. For figures on the different branches of government, see John R. Hibbing and Elizabeth Theiss-Morse, *Congress as Public Enemy: Public Attitudes Toward American Political Institutions* (Cambridge: Cambridge University Press, 1995), 58.

13. Richard F. Fenno, "If, as Ralph Nader Says, Congress Is the 'The Broken Branch,' How Come We Love Our Congressmen So Much?" In Norman J. Ornstein, ed., *Congress in Change: Education and Reform* (New York: Praeger, 1975), 278.

14. On young people's identification of the controlling party see Karl T. Kurtz, Alan Rosenthal, and Cliff Zukin, "Citizenship: A Challenge for All Generations," National Conference of State Legislators, http://www.ncsl.org/public/trust/citizenship.pdf.

15. Cynicism toward politics in general, and neither dissatisfaction with the performance of legislatures nor political ideology, seems responsible for the strong support Americans gave to term limits in the 1990s; see Jeffrey A. Karp, "Explaining Public Support for Legislative Term Limits," *Public Opinion Quarterly* 59 (Autumn 1995), 373–391.

16. Schumpeter, *Capitalism, Socialism, and Democracy,* 272.

17. Hannah Pitkin, *The Concept of Representation* (Berkeley: University of California Press, 1967), 55–57.

18. "Broken Promises: The Death of Deliberative Democracy," compiled by Louise M. Slaughter, 2005, 1.

19. Norman Ornstein and Thomas E. Mann, "If You Give a Congressman a Cookie," *New York Times,* January 19, 2006. See also their book, *The Broken Branch: How Congress Is Failing America and How to Get It Back on Track* (New York: Oxford University Press, 2006).

20. Sidney Verba, "The Citizen as Respondent: Sample Surveys and American Democracy," presidential address, American Political Science Association, 1995, *American Political Science Review* 90 (March 1996), 1, 3. For critiques of Verba's analysis, see Scott L. Althaus, *Collective Preferences in Democratic Politics: Opinion Surveys and the Will of the People* (Cambridge: Cambridge University Press, 2003), and Adam J. Berinksy, *Silent Voices: Political Opinion and Political Participation in America* (Princeton: Princeton University Press, 2004).

21. Alan D. Monroe, "Public Opinion and Public Policy, 1980–1993," *Public Opinion Quarterly* 62 (Spring 1998), 13–14.

22. Respectively, Lawrence R. Jacobs and Robert Y. Shapiro, "The Myth of the Pandering Politician," *Public Perspective* 8 (1997), 3–5; Stephen D. Ansolabehere, James M. Snyder, Jr., and Charles Stewart III, "Candidate Positioning in U.S. House Elections," *American Journal of Political Science* 45 (2001), 136–159.

23. Lawrence R. Jacobs and Robert Y. Shapiro, *Politicians Don't Pander: Political Manipulation and the Loss of Democratic Responsiveness* (Chicago: University of Chicago Press, 2000), xviii.

24. Hibbing and Theiss-Morse, *Stealth Democracy,* 132–133.

25. Cited in Jim VandeHei and Michael A. Fletcher, "Bush Says Election Ratified Iraq Policy: No U.S. Troop Withdrawal Date Is Set," *Washington Post,* January 16, 2005.

Chapter 4.
Democracy Without Institutions

1. Alexis de Tocqueville, *Democracy in America*, trans. Arthur Gold-hammer (New York: Penguin, 2004); Robert Putnam, *Bowling Alone: The Collapse and Revival of American Community* (New York: Simon and Schuster, 2001).

2. I address this individualism in *Moral Freedom: The Search for Virtue in a World of Choice* (New York: Norton, 2001).

3. Sidney M. Milkis, *The President and the Parties: The Transformation of the American Party System Since the New Deal* (New York: Oxford University Press, 1993).

4. The best account of this conservative grassroots organizing is Rick Perlstein, *Before the Storm: Barry Goldwater and the Unmaking of the American Consensus* (New York: Hill and Wang, 2001).

5. Martin P. Wattenberg, *The Rise of Candidate-Centered Politics: Presidential Elections of the 1980s* (Cambridge: Harvard University Press, 1991), 38.

6. Martin P. Wattenberg, *The Decline of American Political Parties, 1952–1994* (Cambridge: Harvard University Press, 1996), 21.

7. Wattenberg, *Rise of Candidate-Centered Politics,* 40.

8. Walter Dean Burnham, *Critical Elections and the Mainsprings of American Politics* (New York: Norton, 1970), 130–131; Gerald Pomper, "Impacts on the Party System," in Samuel Kirkpatrick, ed., *American Electoral Behavior: Change and Stability* (Beverly Hills, Calif.: Sage, 1976), 137. Both are cited in Wattenberg, *Decline of American Political Parties,* 24.

9. Wattenberg, *Rise of Candidate-Centered Politics,* 1. See also John H. Aldrich, *Why Parties? The Origin and Transformation of Political Parties in America* (Chicago: University of Chicago Press, 1995).

10. For a collection of essays arguing along these lines see L. Sandy Meisel, ed., *The Parties Respond: Changes in American Parties and Campaigns* (Boulder, Colo.: Westview, 2002).

11. Alan I. Abramowitz, "The End of the Democratic Era? 1994 and the Future of Congressional Election Research," *Political Research Quarterly* 48 (December 1995), 879.

12. Larry M. Bartels, "Partisanship and Voting Behavior, 1952–1996," *American Journal of Political Science* 44 (January 2000), 35–50.

13. John F. Bibby, "State Party Organizations: Strengthened and Adapting to Candidate-Centered Politics and Nationalization," in Meisel, *Parties Respond,* 19–20.

14. Steven E. Schier, *By Invitation Only: The Rise of Exclusive Politics in the United States* (Pittsburgh: University of Pittsburgh Press, 2000).

15. See Norman Ornstein and Barry McMillion, "One Nation, Divisible," *New York Times,* June 24, 2005.

16. Jeffrey M. Stonecash, Mark D. Brewer, and Mark D. Mariani, *Diverging Parties: Social Change, Realignment, and Party Polarization* (Boulder, Colo.: Westview, 2003).

17. Committee on Political Parties, American Political Science Association, "Toward a More Responsible Two-Party System," *American Political Science Review* 44 (1950), Supplement, 18–19, cited in John C. Green and Paul S. Herrnson, "The Search for Responsibility," in John C. Green and Paul S. Herrnson, eds., *Responsible Partisanship? The Evolution of American Political Parties Since 1950* (Lawrence: University Press of Kansas, 2002), 4.

18. Martin Kady II, "Learning to Stick Together: House Democrats Reached Record Unity in 2005, as the Senate GOP's Loyalties Swayed Slightly," *CQ Weekly,* January 9, 2006, 93.

19. Larry J. Sabato and Bruce Larson, *The Party's Just Begun: Shaping Political Parties for America's Future,* 2nd ed. (New York: Longman, 2002), 5.

20. The classic expression of this purpose can be found in William Kornhauser, *The Politics of Mass Society* (Glencoe, Ill.: Free Press, 1959).

21. John R. Hibbing and Elizabeth Theiss-Morse, *Stealth Democracy: Americans' Beliefs About How Government Should Work* (Cambridge: Cambridge University Press, 2002), 75, 102.

22. E. E. Schattschneider, *The Semi-Sovereign People: A Realist's View of Democracy in America* (Hindsale, Ill.: Dryden, 1975 [1960]); Charles E. Lindblom, *Politics and Markets: The World's Political-Economic Systems* (New York: Basic, 1977).

23. Hibbing and Theiss-Morse, *Stealth Democracy,* 90.

24. Sabato and Lawson, *The Party's Just Begun,* 13–16.

25. For statistics on California, Oregon, and Colorado see Richard J. Ellis, *Democratic Delusions: The Initiative Process in America* (Lawrence: University Press of Kansas, 2002), 38.

26. David Broder, *Democracy Derailed: Initiative Campaigns and the Power of Money* (New York: Harcourt, 2000), 1; Ellis, *Democratic Delusions,* passim.

27. Barbara S., Gamble, "Putting Civil Rights to a Popular Vote," *American Journal of Political Science* 41 (January 1997), 245–269.

28. Stephen P. Nicholson, *Voting the Agenda: Candidates, Elections, and Ballot Propositions* (Princeton: Princeton University Press, 2005).

29. Elisabeth R. Gerber and Arthur Lupia, "Voter Competence in Direct Legislative Elections," in Stephen L. Elkin and Karol Edward Soltan, eds.,

Citizen Competence and Democratic Institutions (University Park: Pennsylvania State University Press, 1999), 147–160.

30. Elisabeth R. Gerber, *The Populist Paradox: Interest Group Influence and the Promise of Direct Legislation* (Princeton: Princeton University Press, 1999).

31. Mark A. Smith, "Ballot Initiatives and the Democratic Citizen," *Journal of Politics* 64 (August 2002), 892–903; Shaun Bowler and Todd Donovan, "Democracy, Institutions, and Attitudes About Citizen Influence on Government," *British Journal of Political Science* 32 (2002), 371–390; Martin Gilens, James Glaser, and Tali Mendelberg, "Having a Say: Political Efficacy in the Context of Direct Democracy," paper presented at the American Political Science Association meetings, August 2001.

32. David H. Everson, "The Effects of Initiatives on Voter Turnout: A Comparative State Analysis," *Western Political Quarterly* 34 (September 1981), 415–425; Mark A. Smith, "The Contingent Effects of Ballot Initiatives and Candidate Races on Turnout," *American Journal of Political Science* 45 (July 2001), 700–706.

33. John G. Matsusaka, *For the Many or the Few: The Initiative, Public Policy, and American Democracy* (Chicago: University of Chicago Press, 2004), xi.

34. Elisabeth R. Gerber, Arthur Lupia, Matthew D. McGubbins, and D. Roderick Kiewiet, *Stealing the Initiative: How State Government Responds to Direct Democracy* (Upper Saddle River, N.J.: Prentice Hall, 2001), 4.

35. Cited in Ellis, *Democratic Delusions,* 200.

Chapter 5.
Democracy Without Disinterest

1. For examples, see L. Brent Bozell, III, *Weapons of Mass Distortion: The Coming Meltdown of the Liberal Media* (New York: Crown Forum, 2004), and Eric Alterman, *What Liberal Media? The Truth About Bias and the News* (New York: Basic, 2003).

2. Quoted in Paul Starr, *The Creation of the Media: Political Origins of Modern Communications* (New York: Basic, 2004), 338.

3. Quoted in James T. Hamilton, *All the News That's Fit to Sell: How the Market Transforms Information into News* (Princeton: Princeton University Press, 2004), 164–165.

4. Ibid., 178, 181.

5. Ibid., 113.

6. Cass Sunstein, *Republic.com* (Princeton: Princeton University Press, 2001), 22.

7. Quoted in Walter Isaacson and Evan Thomas, *The Wise Men: Six Friends and the World They Made* (New York: Simon and Schuster, 1986), 702.

8. David E. Sanger, "Visited by a Host of Administrations, Bush Hears Some Chastening Words," *New York Times*, January 6, 2006.

9. John Judis, *The Paradox of American Democracy: Elites, Special Interests, and the Betrayal of Public Trust* (New York: Pantheon, 2000).

10. John F. Kennedy, Commencement Speech at Yale University, June 11, 1962, http://www.jfklibrary.org/j061162.htm.

11. Gregory Kabaservice, *The Guardians: Kingman Brewster, His Circle, and the Rise of the Liberal Establishment* (New York: Henry Holt, 2004).

12. Judis, *Paradox of American Democracy*, 169.

13. For examples of this kind of thinking, see Herbert Wechsler, "Toward Neutral Principles of Constitutional Law," *Harvard Law Review* 73 (November 1959), 1–35, and Alexander Bickel, *The Least Dangerous Branch: The Supreme Court at the Bar of Politics* (Indianapolis: Bobbs-Merrill, 1962).

14. Ethan Bronner, *Battle for Justice: How the Bork Nomination Shook America* (New York: Norton, 1989).

15. Thomas M. Keck, *The Most Activist Supreme Court in History: The Road to Modern Judicial Conservatism* (Chicago: University of Chicago Press, 2004), 40.

16. *U.S. v. Rybar*, 103 F.3d 273 (3rd. Cir. 1996).

17. Daniel Bell and Irving Kristol, "What Is The Public Interest?" *Public Interest* 1 (Fall 1965), 4.

18. Rep. Henry A. Waxman, "The Content of Federally Funded Abstinence Only Programs," United States House of Representatives, Committee on Government Reform, Minority Staff Investigative Division, December 2004; see also http://democrats.reform.house.gov/features/politics_and_science/example_condoms.htm.

19. On the evidence question, see Judith Stacey and Timothy Biblarz, "(How) Does the Sexual Orientation of Parents Matter?" *American Sociological Review* 66 (April 2001), 159–183.

20. http://democrats.reform.house.gov/features/politics_and_science/example_education.htm.

21. Chris Mooney, *The Republican War on Science* (New York: Perseus, 2005). A more polemical treatment can be found in Esther Kaplan, *With God on Their Side: How Christian Fundamentalists Trampled Science, Policy, and Democracy in George W. Bush's White House* (New York: New Press, 2004).

22. Eli Ginzberg and Robert M. Solow, "Some Lessons of the 1960s," *Public Interest* 34 (Winter 1974), 214–216.

23. For vivid treatments of this and similar examples, see Tamar Jacoby, *Someone Else's House: America's Unfinished Struggle for Integration* (New York: Free Press, 1998), and Fred Siegel, *The Future Once Happened Here: New York, D.C., L.A., and the Fate of America's Big Cities* (New York: Free Press, 1997).

Chapter 6.
Democracy Without Justice

1. Immanuel Kant, *Grounding for the Metaphysics of Morals,* trans. James W. Ellington (Indianapolis: Hackett, 1981 [1785]), 3.

2. See, for example, Brian Barry, *Justice as Impartiality* (New York: Oxford University Press, 1995).

3. Brian Barry, *Why Social Justice Matters* (Cambridge: Polity, 2005), 4.

4. William Graham Sumner, *What Social Classes Owe to Each Other* (New York: Arno, 1972 [1883]).

5. On the New Deal's imperfections, see Ira Katznelson, *When Affirmative Action Was White: An Untold History of Racial Inequality in Twentieth Century America* (New York: Norton, 2005).

6. Barry, *Why Social Justice Matters,* 14.

7. Jacob S. Hacker and Paul Pierson, *Off Center: The Republican Revolution and the Erosion of American Democracy* (New Haven: Yale University Press, 2005), 46.

8. Citizens for Tax Justice, "Year-by-Year Analysis of the Bush Tax Cuts Shows Growing Tilt to the Very Rich," http:/www.ctj.org/html/gwb0602 .htm, cited in Larry M. Bartels, "Homer Gets a Tax Cut: Inequality and Public Policy in the American Mind," *Perspectives on Politics* 3 (March 2005), 16.

9. For a review of poll data indicating support for the cuts, see Bartels, "Homer Gets a Tax Cut," 19–21. For the relative importance of taxation, see Hacker and Pierson, *Off Center,* 50–51.

10. See, for example, the Associated Press poll of March 19–21, 2004, Ipsos Public Affairs, and the Policy Analysis of California Education (PACE) survey of May 2003, http://www.berkeley.edu/news/media/releases/2003/05/ 20_taxcut.shtml.

11. Bartels, "Homer Gets a Tax Cut," 20–21.

12. Arthur Lupia, Adam Seth Levine, Jesse O. Menning, and Gisela Sin, "Were Bush Tax Cut Supporters 'Simply Ignorant'?: A Second Look at Conservatives and Liberals in 'Homer Gets a Tax Cut,'" http://www-personal .umich.edu/~lupia/.

13. Charles Tiefer, *Veering Right: How the Bush Administration Sub-*

verts the Law for Conservative Causes (Berkeley: University of California Press, 2004), 118–119.

14. Pierson and Hacker, *Off Center*.

15. Mary Ann Glendon, *A World Made New: Eleanor Roosevelt and the Universal Declaration of Human Rights* (New York: Random House, 2001), 175. See also Elizabeth Borgwardt, *A New Deal for the World: America's Vision for Human Rights* (Cambridge: Harvard University Press, 2005).

16. Cited in Glendon, *World Made New*, 193.

17. The ideas in this paragraph are indebted to Anatol Lieven, *America Right or Wrong: An Anatomy of American Nationalism* (New York: Oxford University Press, 2004).

18. Schlafly's description can be found in Donald T. Critchlow, *Phyllis Schlafly and Grassroots Conservatism* (Princeton: Princeton University Press, 2005), 176.

19. http://globalization.about.com/library/weekly/aa100302a.htm.

20. The best account of these traditions can be found in Walter Russell Mead, *Special Providence: American Foreign Policy and How It Changed the World* (New York: Knopf, 2001).

21. Samantha Power, *"A Problem from Hell": America and the Age of Genocide* (New York: Perseus, 2002), 503. Emphasis in the original.

22. Condoleezza Rice, "Promoting the National Interest," *Foreign Affairs* 79 (January–February 2000), 53, cited in James M. McCormick, "The Foreign Policy of the George W. Bush Administration," in Steven E. Schier, ed., *High Risk and Big Ambition: The Presidency of George W. Bush* (Pittsburgh: University of Pittsburgh Press, 2004), 196.

23. Mark Danner, *Torture and Truth: America, Abu Ghraib, and the War on Terror* (New York: New York Review of Books, 2004); Karen J. Greenberg and Joshua Dratel, *The Torture Papers* (New York: Cambridge University Press, 2005).

24. Ian Shapiro, *Democratic Justice* (New Haven: Yale University Press, 1999).

25. Richard J. Arneson, "Democracy Is Not Intrinsically Just," in Keith Dowding, Robert E. Goodin, and Carole Pateman, eds., *Justice and Democracy: Essays for Brian Barry* (Cambridge: Cambridge University Press, 2004), 40–58.

Chapter 7.
The Rise of Conservative Democracy

1. For an argument along these lines, see Mark Crispin Miller, *Cruel and Unusual: Bush/Cheney's New World Order* (New York: Norton, 2004).

2. Fareed Zakaria, *The Future of Freedom: Illiberal Democracy at Home and Abroad* (New York: Norton, 2003), 116.

3. My understanding of liberalism's major principles has been shaped by Stephen Holmes, *Passions and Constraints: On the Theory of Liberal Democracy* (Chicago: University of Chicago Press, 1995).

4. Two general statements of this point of view can be found in Alasdair MacIntyre, *After Virtue: A Study in Moral Theory* (Notre Dame: University of Notre Dame Press, 1981), and Stanley Fish, *The Trouble with Principle* (Cambridge: Harvard University Press, 1999). For an application to a specific issue, see Winnifred Fallers Sullivan, *The Impossibility of Religious Freedom* (Princeton: Princeton University Press, 2005).

5. For recent treatments of how the Enlightenment influenced America's political founders, see Darren Staloff, *Hamilton, Adams, Jefferson: The Politics of Enlightenment and the American Founding* (New York: Hill and Wang, 2005), and David L. Holmes, *The Faiths of the Founding Fathers* (New York: Oxford University Press, 2006).

6. Norbert Elias, *The Civilizing Process: The History of Manners,* trans. Edmund Jephcott (New York: Urizen, 1978 [1939]).

7. Elizabeth Anne Oldmixon, *Uncompromising Positions: God, Sex, and the U.S. House of Representatives* (Washington, D.C.: Georgetown University Press, 2005).

8. Lewis L. Gould, *The Most Exclusive Club: A Modern History of the United States Senate* (New York: Perseus, 2005), 318.

9. The best account of Rove's career and tactics can be found in Joshua Green, "Karl Rove in a Corner," *Atlantic Monthly* 294 (November 2004), 92–102.

10. As cited by David Ignatius, "The Party of Performance," *Washington Post,* September 9, 2005.

Index

voter distrust + frustration
↓
not working w/in system to beat
system
* pg 97 tyranny of the majority, but ~~the~~
not only
base ~~the~~ emotions of the public
new politics, new media

naïveté on part of citizens
~~governments~~ ~~????~~
~~verbal ff~~
unrealistic expectations from
politicians

led by people who are quite
removed from the majority of the
populace

What is the development or the
causation for new breed of
politicians. W/ new democracy
there more than likely is a
new political actor

Public wants something for nothing
want govt to be the way they'd
like to ~~see~~ it, but ~~they~~ are
unwilling to contribute to be a
catalyst for it

Voter turnout, incumbency, electoral system
(college) futile feeling (2000 presidential
election)

Rise in Executive/President Powers
and Judicial Powers, meanwhile
there ● has been an abdication
of powers/authority by the
Legislative Branch especially
Congress - which is the most
democratic arm in govt.